C000216265

Whether through one of our chat
his great books, I have learned s
being more calm and focused and
on the right things to do and whe
them done. Like everyone, I can easily fall into the urgency
trap, reacting to what is always more demand than I'll ever
be able to supply. But it's Dermot's advice and techniques that
make this urgency whirlwind happen less and less often. As the
world continues to change around us, businesses can't afford to
give in to the urgency trap anymore. We all need to get more
focused and deliberate on deciding the right things to do and
when to do them, and then get them done. And Dermot's book,
Urgent!, is the practical formula to help us.

Stacey Barr, strategic performance specialist,
author of *Prove it!*

This latest offering from Australia's leading expert
on productivity is his best work yet (and that's saying
something...Dermot's work as already had a profound impact
on me and my team, and transformed how we work and how
we work together). If you want to do more deep work, more
meaningful work and have an impact, the key is taming urgency.
As you'll learn, we don't want to eradicate urgency (as if we
could)...just get rid of unproductive urgency and fuel ourselves
with the right kind or urgency at the right time. This book will
show you how. You'll finish this book with deep clarity about
what to do and energised to take action. This is the thinking
person's productivity bible for the next decade.

Peter Cook, Chairperson of Thought Leaders,
author of *The Thought Leaders Practice* and
The New Rules of Management

Disruption requires us to deal with immediacy, but that does not mean everything requires urgency. This book explains the difference.

Matt Church, founder of Thought Leaders Global, author of *Amplifiers*

COVID-19 showed us that we can all work differently. It forced us to reassess what was urgent, what was important and what was a true crisis. Dermot Crowley's latest book *Urgent!* points out the 'inconvenient truth' of urgent work and how this leads to unproductive cultures. *Urgent!* shows us how to be less reactive and more productive by learning to moderate urgency.

Gabrielle Dolan, author of *Real Communication* and *Stories for Work*

Dermot has been guiding our team through 'Smart Work' and 'Smart Teams' for just over two years. The strength and clarity of his knowledge and personal work practices flow into his books and training, and our results have been transformational. Team members experience a much greater sense of control and ease in their work days, and together we have adopted a shared 'productivity' language and culture.

Lesley Mackay, GM Tasmania, The Smith Family

Told with genuine insight and a sprinkle of wit, never could this evidence-based study be any more timely and urgent than now, in this era of shifting and resetting workplace paradigms. An easy-to-follow playbook for business and government leaders and workers to make sense of what we do today but should be doing tomorrow.

Charles Miranda, author, editor and journalist

URGENT!

URGENT!

STRATEGIES TO CONTROL URGENCY, REDUCE STRESS AND INCREASE PRODUCTIVITY

DERMOT CROWLEY

WILEY

First published in 2020 by John Wiley & Sons Australia, Ltd
42 McDougall St, Milton Qld 4064

Office also in Melbourne

Typeset in Crimson Text Regular 12/15pt

© John Wiley & Sons Australia, Ltd 2020

The moral rights of the author have been asserted

ISBN: 978-0-730-38465-6

A catalogue record for this book is available from the National Library of Australia

Cover design by Wiley

Cover image © Thomas Pajot / Getty Images

Printed in Singapore by Markono Print Media Pte Ltd

10 9 8 7 6 5 4 3 2 1

Disclaimer
The material in this publication is of the nature of general comment only, and does not represent professional advice. It is not intended to provide specific guidance for particular circumstances and it should not be relied on as the basis for any decision to take action or not take action on any matter which it covers. Readers should obtain professional advice where appropriate, before making any such decision. To the maximum extent permitted by law, the author and publisher disclaim all responsibility and liability to any person, arising directly or indirectly from any person taking or not taking action based on the information in this publication.

For my brother Donal — a great man who was never in a hurry but left us all too quickly.

Contents

About the author

Dermot Crowley's passion is productivity and helping individuals and organisations to work more productively. He has more than 25 years' experience in the productivity training industry where he has worked as an author, speaker, trainer and thought leader. He has run his own business, Adapt Productivity, since 2002. He is the author of *Smart Work*, published by John Wiley in 2016, and *Smart Teams*, also published by Wiley in 2018.

Dermot was born in Dublin, Ireland, and moved in 1993 to Sydney, Australia, where he now lives and works. When not writing books, you can find Dermot working with some of Australia's leading companies, as well as travelling the globe for his international clients. In between these engagements you will find him in the kitchen, in coffee shops and sometimes in trouble!

You can also find him at **www.adaptproductivity.com.au**.

Acknowledgements

As always, so many people to thank. My fingers may have done the typing, and my brain may have done the thinking, but I stood on the shoulders of some, and leaned on the shoulders of others over the past few months.

Firstly, a huge thanks to my beautiful partner Vera, who has an unshakeable faith in my ability and my value. Grazie, bella. Ti voglio bene. To my son Finn, who graciously puts up with my references to him in my books, and the stories that he invariably ends up starring in. I talk about him a lot, but I am a dad who cannot help himself. Finn, you are my inspiration.

To my team at Adapt: Chauntelle, Tony and Matt. I resisted having a team for so many years, because I thought I could do it all by myself. How wrong I was, and how lucky I am to have you at my back, and by my side.

As always thank you to my Thought Leaders tribe, especially Matt and Pete. There are many thought leaders who have helped shape my thinking for this book, and you all inspire me to be better every day.

A big thank you to Professor Ron Heifetz and his team at the Harvard Kennedy Business School. You inspired this book, and I hope it does justice to your great thinking.

Thanks to all of my clients who not only contributed their philosophies and learnings to this book, but also the ones with whom I have worked over the past twenty years. You have all contributed in some way to my thinking.

Kelly Irving has been the one who has whipped my books into shape in the early stages for a few years now. As always, thank you for tolerating my messy drafts and extended deadlines.

Finally thank you to the team at Wiley. Book number three — we have to stop meeting like this! Lucy, Chris and Ali, you have all helped to bring this to life. Thank you for your faith and guidance.

And of course, I should not forget you, dear reader. You have picked this book up and started reading it, even though you probably have many more urgent things to do. That is legendary! Enjoy.

A note from the author

June 2019

As I write this, I'm overlooking the beach in Monterosso, an achingly beautiful town in Liguria. Think rugged coastline, views to die for, painted villages and the home of pesto. The pace of life in Monterosso is slow — delightfully slow.

It might seem strange to be writing a book on urgency in such a non-urgent place. Right now, I have absolutely zero urgency in my world. I don't have any client delivery for another couple of weeks. My team have things handled very well back home. In fact, my most pressing issue right now is whether to have a beer or an Aperol spritz before dinner. And even that decision is not all that pressing — it's currently 3 pm.[1]

But maybe the best time to start a book on urgency is when you are removed from it. When you can objectively think about how and why urgency arises and the impact that it has on our work and our lives. Perhaps it is the perfect time to reflect on the stories that we tell ourselves about how urgency is just a

---

[1] I ended up having an Aperol spritz, and then a beer. At 4 pm. Is that bad?

normal by-product of modern life; that there is nothing to be done about it and this is 'just the way it is around here'.

But while something urgent cropping up seems unlikely for me now, that could change at any moment.

I could step on a piece of glass on the beach and end up in the emergency ward. (I hope I won't, but it is possible.) I could get a call from a client chasing some information I had promised but forgot to send. (I am confident that won't happen!) I could be asked to join George Clooney on his boat on Lake Como if I can just get there by 8 pm tonight. (I am positive this won't happen.)

Many things could arise that would create urgency in my world, but while I would like to be able to respond to any of these situations, I do not feel the need to be in a reactive state 'just in case' they do. And if they do happen, I would hope that I'd deal with the situation with the appropriate level of response.

This subtle but important difference between responsiveness and reactivity is what this book will explore. It may require a shift in mindset for you, or even a shift in culture for your organisation. But both these things can be done — with a little effort. Unfortunately, sometimes we can feel we are powerless to change things in our workplace.

Due to the increased pace of business, and the constant flow of information, many of us have adopted victim mindsets when it comes to urgency. We become the victims of urgency and feel there is little we can do to reduce the reactivity in our workplace. We just accept it as normal. But there is plenty we can do, both at a personal productivity level and at a cultural level within our teams and organisations.

Not only can we do something about the urgency that drives most of our time and effort, we absolutely *must* do something about it.

Urgency, or more accurately the toxic urgency that comes from acute and chronic periods of reactivity, is one of the most destructive forces in any organisation. It can derail productivity, sap morale and burn people out.

They say that people don't leave organisations; they leave bad managers. Well I believe that they also leave bad cultures, and permanently reactive cultures are hard to live with for long periods. So I would like to help minimise this reactivity.

But here is the challenge. Urgency is also a useful tool, and without it, we would struggle to gain traction with important initiatives, deliver client work on time or meet business obligations. Most senior managers use urgency as a lever to drive work forward, and would potentially resist having people like me come in preaching a slower, more casual way of operating.

But the solution to this problem is not to take an opposite extreme position and slow right down; the solution lies in dialling down the urgency to a more sustainable level. A level where the urgency is neither acute (very strong) nor chronic (very long). A level where urgency is a useful tool that can be used in a measured and purposeful way, by everyone in the team. This is what I call moderated urgency, and I think you will find it a useful concept in many areas of your life.

Don't you feel that life has got crazy busy, both at home and at work? We are always rushing around from one place to another, one meeting to another, one email to another! We are constantly distracted by our screens and the stream of updates from the people around us. As a society we don't relax like we used to—and yet can we truly say that this increase in busy-ness has delivered better outcomes? I don't think so. The urgency problem is not the cause of all of this, but it is definitely a central theme. This is why I felt compelled to write this book.

So if urgency has become your new normal, then this book is for you. If your team or organisation constantly operates in a reactive haze of deadlines, last-minute meetings and fire-fighting, read on and give a copy of this book to your leadership team. If you are inspired to do great work, but feel constantly frustrated by the issues and supposed crises that crop up every day, I hope you take hope from this book. I encourage you to take some small steps towards creating a less reactive, yet more productive workplace for you and your colleagues.

Phew. A lot of thoughts for my little brain. Time for a swim and another one of those excellent spritzes, I reckon. I'll enjoy that while you enjoy the book. Take your time with it, though. There's no hurry.

April 2020

As I put the finishing touches on this book, we are all coming to terms with the severity of the Coronavirus crisis. We are dealing with living in self-isolation and having our personal and professional lives completely disrupted. This is an event that has touched every one of us, and completely changed how we live, work and think. The COVID-19 pandemic has given us all a new perspective on what is truly urgent.

This is a situation that I did not foresee when I was sipping my drink in Monterosso. It is a situation that none of us could have foreseen. While a highly-trained professional would have planned for something like this, everyday workers like you and I could never have conceived of this happening outside of the movies, and therefore could never have been expected to plan for it.

For some of us, the crisis has thrown our world into chaos and has meant we have had to deal with many urgent and unexpected issues. Our priorities a month ago are not the same as our priorities today. And that is part of what this book aims to help you with: how to respond when truly urgent things demand your attention.

But I believe that something else is happening in the minds of millions of workers around the globe that will have a lasting impact on our relationship to urgency. As we now try to do our work in a totally different mental context and physical environment, many of us are resetting.

You may have concluded that the way you had been working was a bit unrealistic and unsustainable. Now that you cannot physically meet with others because of self-isolation requirements, you may have realised you were spending too much of your time in meetings anyway. As you work from home rather than the office, you may be surprised at how focused you can be without the constant interruptions of an open-plan workspace. And as you focus on the critical activities that you need to do to help your business survive, you may have realised that so much of your time pre-COVID-19 was spent reacting to things that may not have mattered much after all.

We are currently going through the greatest challenge of our time. As you read this, hopefully we have passed through the worst of the crises. But I have no doubt we will still be dealing with the aftermath. I am personally devastated by what has unfolded. But I am also very optimistic that once this is over, we will have reset in many ways and will be open to new ways of living and working. So, here's to a brave new world, one that is just a little less reactive, and a little more driven by what is truly important.

Dermot Crowley

Introduction

How does urgency affect our work and results? What causes so much urgency and reactivity in our workplace? Why has the pace of business accelerated so much over the past few years? And how do we learn to use urgency purposefully to ensure we deliver meaningful work in a timely way, rather than running around in a panicked frenzy? These are all questions we need to explore if we are going to harness urgency to drive us forward, instead of struggling against a headwind of constant urgency that makes progress harder than it needs to be.

Urgency is a reality in our modern workplace. But of course, not all urgency is within our control. Nor is all urgency bad; some things are impossible to plan for. Most of us are working in roles with many moving parts, balancing everyday issues with more complex initiatives. It's complicated.

Consider a project. A project is a proactive endeavour that in a perfect world would have minimal urgency associated with it. If you are clear about the outcome to be achieved, and you plan the project well, and you estimate the duration of each activity effectively, and everyone does what they need to do when they need to do it, and you have no unexpected issues or delays, and you are not distracted by other work or issues, and nobody gets sick, and the world decides to work with you and not against you, then you might sail through the project with minimal urgency and reactivity. But that is unrealistic. Life is messy. Projects are complicated. People are busy and overwhelmed.

Urgency, when used appropriately, can create traction, build momentum and get things done. Urgency helps us to overcome inertia and complacency. But if used inappropriately, it can also distract us from other important priorities, waste time and resources, and burn people out.

We have to expect a certain amount of urgency in life. I'm not suggesting we can eradicate urgency, but we can minimise *unproductive* urgency. This is the urgency that could have been avoided in the first place. The unnecessary urgency that creates stress and slows work down. The urgency that can become a toxic part of your culture, and then become the norm.

Why are we in so much of a hurry these days?

My father, also named Dermot Crowley, was the head accountant for the ESB, or Electricity Supply Board, in Ireland. It was a senior role, but it never seemed to be a busy one, at least not by today's senior executive standard.[2] Dad had a big office, and I loved visiting him with my mum when we were in the

---

[2] At least to an eight-year-old. Maybe if I was eight years old today and visited a large corporate workplace, nobody would seem busy either. I doubt it though.

city shopping before Christmas, or when we were going to a show or the movies. This would have been in the 1970s, when I was about eight years old.

I remember being led into his office by his secretary, and it seemed like a whole floor to me. It was huge to a small boy, with a big desk and a meeting table. My favourite thing in Dad's office was his cheque-signing machine. Because he had to sign every wages cheque in the organisation, he had a machine that printed his signature onto the cheque. (This was in the days before personal computers.) The signing machine was kept in a huge safe in his office, and it was all very James Bond to me.

Despite the impressiveness of the surroundings, Dad never seemed that busy, and was never in a hurry! He always had a clear desk, and always had the time to meet us for lunch. In fact, he always took lunch. Later on, he would have lunch in the staff canteen, but when I was really young he would drive home for lunch (about twenty minutes each way). He would start work at 9 am and be home by 5.30 pm, which must have meant he left the office at 5 pm.

Imagine that nowadays! A senior executive who starts at 9 am and finishes at 5 pm, and has time for lunch each day! It seems impossible to most. But back then it was a different time. It just wasn't as busy. People did not have the same relentless pressures on them. They didn't attend as many meetings. They certainly didn't have the volume of emails to contend with on top of everything else.

What has happened over the last few decades? Are our priorities so much more important now? Are things so much more urgent now because business has changed? Or have *we* changed, and just allowed the pace of business to get faster and faster, and told ourselves stories about how this increased pace has led to better outcomes?

To my mind, urgency has increased in our workplaces because of one crucial innovation that has changed the way that we work and the way we live. *Technology.* In my father's day, computers were just coming into the workplace, but in the form of large mainframe systems in big rooms, not laptops on each desk. But of course, today's workplace is radically different because of technology.

Technology has sped the world up, and this shows itself in numerous ways:

- communication technologies such as email have shortened the time it takes to communicate a message to others

- the ability to easily communicate across geographically spread offices means that someone is always working and requiring work from us

- the ubiquity of laptops, tablets and smartphones makes us contactable at any time, in any place

- the expectation of instant gratification driven by tools such as social media and online shopping has bled into our workstyles

- technology-driven media ensures that issues that affect our organisations are very public, very quickly

- technology that has enabled faster product development cycles that require speedy innovation to stay relevant and profitable.

Now, I love technology, and in fact have built a business around leveraging technology to help people stay organised. I believe that, overall, the impact of technology has been incredibly positive, and even the ways that technology has increased the pace of business are not necessarily bad. They are just a reality that we need to acknowledge and be aware of.

This change in the working landscape has not just led to us being busier and more reactive as individuals. I believe it has changed the very cultures we work in and, unfortunately, how our organisations are led. Many of us now work in overly reactive cultures with leaders who struggle to deal with the issues that arise from this faster pace of business.

The reality is that the fish rots from the head down, so reactive cultures can often be caused by reactive leaders.

If you are a manager or a leader, this might not be a comfortable statement for you. Just like Al Gore called climate change science an 'inconvenient truth' for governments, I call urgent cultures an inconvenient truth for leadership teams. Leaders are a part of the problem. Too often, in my experience, they use urgency as a blunt instrument to drive work forward. If leaders are not directly causing the urgency, they may be turning a blind eye to the long-term effects of acute and chronic reactivity. And I believe that this is having an incredibly negative impact on the workforce.

One of the key reasons I decided to write this book was to raise awareness of this issue for leadership teams, and, dare I say, create an urgency focus on addressing this issue in their organisation. The challenge I faced was that if I suggested to a leadership team that they 'dial down the urgency', they would usually push right back and say, 'Hold on, we need our people to be working with a sense of urgency. That's how we get traction and drive important work forward.' However, this paradigm shifted for me earlier this year on a trip to the United States.

The urgency trap

I have been thinking about the problem of urgency for many years, but always struggled to find the right frame to discuss urgency and its associated problems. Then in 2019, I spent some time at Harvard, studying under Professor Ron Heifetz, a leading thinker in the field of leadership.[3] Listening to Ron and his team, it dawned on me that there may be a way to deal with the urgency problem without just slowing work down. Leaders and managers need to help their teams to moderate urgency and use it in a more meaningful way. They need to help their teams to avoid the urgency trap.

The urgency trap is where we end up working with too much or not enough urgency. Leaders and managers should aim to apply just the right amount of urgency in a purposeful way to get things done on time.

Remember, not all urgency is bad. The negative effects of urgency can be minimised if we learn to use urgency with a sense of purpose. That is, to use it when required but to use it sparingly.

This is easier said than done.

---

[3] I talk a bit more about Ron's work later on.

As we work, different demands and pressures will present themselves. Most of us have lots of things to do and may have a busy meeting schedule to juggle alongside a list of priorities demanding our attention. Most of us are struggling to keep up.

If you are leading people you will need to manage this dilemma both for yourself and for your team. Of course, you need to keep work moving forward, making sure deadlines are met and issues are dealt with in a timely way. But what happens when everything becomes urgent, and your team start getting overwhelmed? Or if they switch off, or burn out and grind to a halt?

Urgency forces us into unproductive zones if we are not careful. In fact, there are three zones in which we operate as we do our work:

1. reactive

2. active

3. inactive.

Figure A (overleaf) helps us understand the different types of urgency we deal with and how this affects us.

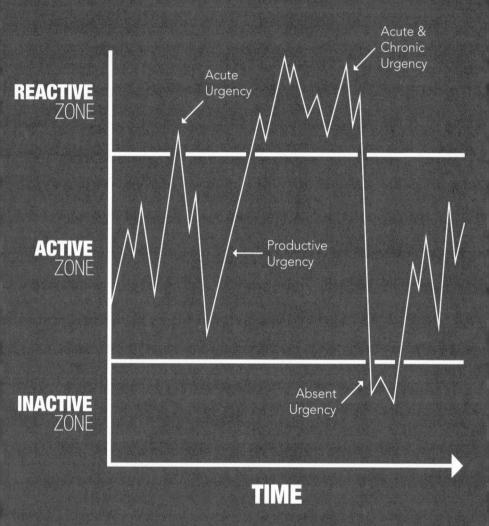

REACTIVE ZONE

ACTIVE ZONE

INACTIVE ZONE

Acute Urgency

Acute & Chronic Urgency

Productive Urgency

Absent Urgency

TIME

Figure A: urgency zones

The reactive zone

The reactive zone is hot and uncomfortable, and can cause all sorts of issues if we work here too often, and for too long. When we are forced into this zone, urgency becomes acute,[4] and there is pressure to react and get it done. Acute urgency in itself is not a problem. Urgency, as long as it is reasonable and reasonably short, is good, and actually helps to create traction and momentum. The problem comes when urgency becomes both acute (very strong) and chronic (very long). Long periods of urgent pressure have a detrimental effect on workers. If everything is urgent in a worker's day or week, things start to get hard and people begin to get stressed and burn out.

A lot of teams and organisations operate in the reactive zone for extended periods, and they don't even realise it. It just becomes the norm, and while at some level they don't like it and complain about it, at another level they feel that they have no choice in the matter. Even when they come down from this heightened state, they can find themselves spiking back up above the line into the reactive zone again very easily. In fact, all too easily! Let me explain with a personal story.

I had the opportunity to go on an amazing trip with my son Finn to Lord Howe Island, off the coast of NSW in Australia. This is a very special place. It is all that is left of a massive submerged volcano, with the remaining rim forming dramatic mountains that rise out of the sea. It has been given World Heritage Status by UNESCO, and only about 400 tourists are allowed to stay on the island at any one time.

---

[4] The Macquarie Dictionary describes acute as 'Sharp in effect; Intense'. I like to describe it as 'very strong', as you will see.

One of the drawcards for Finn and I was to climb Mount Gower, a 900-metre peak at one end of the island. We do not have mountain-climbing skills, but this only requires a very steep guided hike to the top. I say 'only' with my tongue firmly in my cheek. It was the scariest thing I have ever done! But it is part of a father–son ritual that has developed between us. A few years ago, we climbed the highest mountain in Ireland, Carrauntoohil,[5] and since then we've tried to do a challenging walk or climb together each year. This is all the more challenging for me, as I'm desperately afraid of heights. But I push myself to overcome my fear each year, and I believe we have created a very special bond through this ritual. Finn, of course, finds it hilarious to watch me tremble with fear as we begin to ascend. But he also helps me when it gets really bad, and I always make it through without backing out.

So, on this hike we were in a group of about 12 walkers. Our guide was Dean, who had grown up on the island and had been climbing Mount Gower since he was a kid. After trekking for a while on flat ground, we made our way up the side of a cliff to a ledge that was about 100 metres above the sea and ran for about 500 metres. As we crossed the ledge, my fear kicked in, but fortunately there was a rope anchored to the cliff that we could hold for safety, and I managed to cross without too much difficulty (albeit a bit slower than the rest of the group).

We trekked on for another kilometre, and then came the real climb. The next part ascended about 800 metres in the space of 1 kilometre! It was very steep and very tiring, but mostly in forest, so not too challenging for my acrophobia. But I knew the worst part was to come. At about the 800-metre mark,

---

[5] More about Carrauntoohil later.

there was a cliff face that had to be climbed using ropes. It was not very long, but it was very high and very exposed, looking out over the sea almost a kilometre down.

I had agreed to this expedition with the thought that I could always stop at this point and wait for everyone to ascend and come back down again. But Dean, our intrepid guide, had a little chat with me, and told me I could do it, and he would help me get through it. So off we went, up the cliff, my knuckles bleeding from holding the rope so tight against the cliff face. But in a few minutes, we were at the top, and what a sight. Well worth the challenge.

After some lunch and a rest, down we went again. The climb down the cliff was even harder for me than the climb up, and by this stage my body had been in a state of heightened anxiety for quite a few hours. But once we got to the base of the cliff I started to feel a sense of relief. All that was left was the long trek down through the trees, and then the 500-metre cliff ledge, which I had already done without too much trouble, so we were home and hosed as far as I was concerned.

Maybe not! As we got closer to the ledge again, my anxiety began to rise dramatically. I realised that having been in a state of heightened anxiety for so long, my panic was lurking just below the surface, ready to spike up again as soon as I was challenged. And because of this, the thought of the final crossing terrified me. But I had no choice, as it was the only way home. So off I went, again with Dean helping me every step, but this time I almost crawled on my hands and knees, holding on to the side rope like my life depended on it.[6] Dean was patient with me, and stayed behind me every step of the way. We got there in the end and I was incredibly proud of myself, and Finn was very

[6] It actually did!

proud of his dad. A good day all round. I enjoyed my beer that night, I can tell you!

Being in a constant state of urgency and reactivity is just like being in a constant state of anxiety. Even if things quieten down a bit, you can find yourself spiking up quickly into the reactive zone, and sometimes for no good reason. You are just so wired from your previous exposures. I should not have been so scared walking the ledge the second time around. I had already done it and knew I could do it. But I was wired. In the workplace, this wired state is not good for our wellbeing, and can lead to feelings of stress and overwhelm.

Team managers need to be able to identify when this is happening to their people.

Managers need to learn to spot excessive urgency and bring their people back down into the active zone.

They also need to help their team avoid falling into the inactive zone, especially after a period of working on highly urgent deadlines.

As individuals, we need to become more aware of when we are spending too much time in the reactive zone. And we need to engage strategies to get out of this zone, or avoid it in the first place.

The inactive zone

This is the zone where not a lot happens. This is where we coast, not treating anything with a sense of urgency, instead choosing to procrastinate and leave work until later. It is the zone people escape to when they burn out. When the pressure gets too great, we find ourselves unable to move forward, and sometimes just stop. This could show up as people keeping busy doing easy but less meaningful activities such as email, while avoiding their more important work. It could also show up as sick leave or illness, or maybe just a switching off as people deal with the burnout. Unfortunately, to others this may seem like complacency, although often it is not.

When people go to the inactive zone, it is usually not that they are lazy. (Sometimes this is true, but this is the exception rather than the rule.) It is more often a result of working in the reactive zone for too long.

One of my roles is to deliver training courses for clients. It can be quite intense and draining if I have to deliver several days in a row. My first non-delivery day after such a period is often filled with mindless activities. For me this can be a great way to regroup, but it can be unproductive if I stay here for too long.

Again, team managers need to notice when others are in the inactive zone, and get to the bottom of what is causing it. And at a personal level, we need to recognise that too much time spent in the inactive zone can have a range of negative consequences.

The active zone

The active zone is where the best work gets done, and people are at their most effective. I call this the 'Goldilocks zone', a zone that is not too hot and not too cold; it's just right for productive work to be achieved.

Urgency requires us to find the Goldilocks zone—not too reactive, not too inactive, just right.

In this zone there is enough urgency to get traction and momentum with our work, but not so much that it feels like a problem. The pressure will fluctuate over time, but at least workers will have the ability to catch their breath before the next push. Working in this zone has a much more balanced feel, and people are more energised and excited about their work.

Individuals and teams who learn to spend most of their time in the active zone are better able to moderate urgency in a way that serves their work and those around them. They are able to dial up the urgency when needed, and dial it down again when not. They become much more aware of the reactivity around them, and how to manage it.

Moderating urgency

The trick for managers and workers is to step back and watch what is happening, noticing if they or their team are drifting beyond acceptable boundaries because of the presence of, or lack of, urgency. This is what I call *moderating urgency*—making the necessary adjustments to keep working productively in a sustainable way. It's like keeping in your lane when driving: you can do it, but it requires constant attention and adjustment.

Now, I can hear your inner voice saying, 'But I don't have time to constantly monitor and adjust another thing for me or my team!' I know, and I get that. But we will look at strategies that do not take too much of your time or focus. And I can promise you that the time you will save through decreased reactivity and burnout will be worth the effort.

I had a conversation about urgency in a large organisation with an old client, David Koczkar, who is the chief customer officer at Medibank in Australia. David talked about what they call 'sustainable urgency', and their drive to spot and manage unsustainable urgency within the organisation. He monitors this by how people behave in the lift: people who say they are busy but are visibly full of energy work with sustainable urgency. The ones who say they are busy but avoid eye contact at all costs are the ones he worries about, as they are at risk of burning out.

For Medibank, sustainable urgency is all about working out how to hold an appropriate pace that moves things forward without burning people and teams out. How close to the wind can they sail without collapsing the mainsail?[7]

So, what are the strategies available to leaders and managers to help them moderate urgency at this high level, and create more proactive cultures within their organisation?

Part II of this book explores strategies for individuals and managers to moderate urgency. But I will share one strategy with you now, as this concept and tool will thread its way right through the book, and I believe it forms the scaffold upon which we can build our strategies. It is a set of principles that I call the Urgency Playbook.

The Urgency Playbook

In 2011, Chris Anderson, a TED curator, and Jane Wulf, a TED scribe, wrote a blog post on their frustrations with email as a communication tool. This hit a nerve and quickly went viral. It resulted in them creating 'The Email Charter: 10 Rules to Reverse the Email Spiral'. This simple set of common-sense

---

[7] This is a sailing term, as you probably guessed, and refers to sailing into the wind. There is a point where if you get the angle wrong, your sail collapses and you lose speed.

email protocols has become a guide for many people who have become frustrated with the negative impact that high volumes of poor-quality emails have on their productivity.

The email charter was an attempt to help teams create a better email culture by agreeing to some simple group behaviours. It is not an instant fix; it requires leadership, commitment and accountability to work. But initiatives like these can make a big difference to how a team works, and can having a lasting impact on the culture of the team.

Inspired by this, I set about creating what I call the Urgency Playbook. This is simply a set of strategies and principles that we can all agree to that will help us work together more productively in relation to urgency. Playbooks are traditionally associated with American football, but are also used to document how businesses deal with certain activities or situations.

In *Smart Teams,* I wrote about the idea of creating bespoke team agreements to reduce productivity friction. I reckon that working agreements bridge the gap between our good intentions and our actual behaviours. And our behaviours inform the culture of our team.

But in this case I feel that we don't need to reinvent the wheel and create bespoke agreements. I believe that the Urgency Playbook will serve most teams and can become an effective reference document to keep everyone accountable.

As you move through the book, you will learn how to implement the Urgency Playbook in different situations. Each of the ten principles are expanded on at the end of each chapter.[8]

---

[8] You can also download a copy of the playbook at www.urgentbook.com.

THE URGENCY PLAYBOOK

*We agree as a team to adopt this set of common-sense principles
so we can all work together with less stress and disruption.*

1. **Don't cry wolf.**
   Don't make work out to be urgent if it is not, or more
   urgent than it needs to be.

2. **Use urgency with care.**
   Use urgency in a mindful, thoughtful and responsible
   way in order to minimise the negative impact on those
   around you.

3. **Avoid creating unnecessary urgency for others.**
   Don't leave things until the last minute, creating
   unnecessary urgency for others.

4. **Tell them when you need it by.**
   Always clearly state the due date or deadline when
   requesting work.

5. **Don't always expect instant service.**
   Have reasonable expectations around deadlines with
   your team, colleagues and peers.

6. **Use appropriate tools for urgent requests.**
   Avoid using tools like email as the only way to
   communicate urgent requests.

7. **Be responsive, not reactive.**
   Don't just react mindlessly to incoming work, emails and
   communications.

8. **Minimise distraction when interrupting others.**
   Interrupt others in a mindful and purposeful way to
   minimise unnecessary distractions.

9. **Commit fully when it is truly urgent.**
   When a truly urgent issue or opportunity comes along,
   commit fully in your response.

10. **Do what you say you are going to do.**
    Deliver on your promises and commitments, and don't
    force others to chase you up.

Everyone has a role to play

Finally, before we get stuck in, a quick thought on each of the roles we play in using the Urgency Playbook. This book is primarily targeted at managers and team leaders. This is because I firmly believe they are the ones who not only face the most urgency, fielding it from both above and below, but they are also in the best position to moderate urgency across a wider group. That said, we all have a role to play in moderating urgency, and in bringing tools like the Urgency Playbook to life. Whether you are a worker, manager or a leader, you need to get involved if you want to create a more proactive workplace.

Workers

Key focus: Work proactively

As individuals, each of us must take ownership and responsibility around our approach to urgency. We must work proactively whenever possible and be accountable for our actions. This requires building our awareness around our workstyle and habits, and actively managing how we work to minimise unproductive urgency.

In part II particularly, we focus on strategies to help individuals manage their own personal productivity and work more proactively. And this section is not just relevant to team members—managers and leaders are workers too, and must also manage urgency at a personal level.

Managers

Key focus: Moderate urgency

I believe that managers and team leaders are best placed to moderate urgency for themselves and their teams, but it requires managing both up and down.

Managers need to evolve a set of skills that can both protect the team from unnecessary urgency, and also drive urgency when needed. They need a heightened sense of awareness so they can spot reactivity when it occurs, as well as confident negotiation skills to allow them to manage the expectations of those creating urgency for the team.

If I were to choose an avatar to write this book to, it would be a team manager in a medium to large organisation, as they are perfectly placed to take the concepts from this book and apply them. That said, though the bulk of the strategies I discuss are framed in terms of managers, they are all relevant to everyone. Remember, leaders are managers too, and workers may be managers someday.

Leaders
Key focus: Build culture

Leaders hold the power that is needed to change the culture within teams and organisations. I believe that leaders need to see urgency as a cultural issue, and should take responsibility for creating a positive urgency culture. That means opening the space to talk about it, and setting expectations about how urgency is used within the organisation.

So if you are a people leader, read this book with one eye on your own behaviours, one eye on moderating urgency at the team level, and one eye on how you can create sustained cultural change around urgency and reactivity for your wider organisation.[9]

So, now that we've set the scene, let's have a good look at urgency so we can understand what it really is.

---

[9] Please be assured that I am not suggesting that the leaders in your organisation are weird alien beasts with three eyes. You know what I mean!

PART I
Understanding Urgency

Most workplaces are driven by urgency and, unfortunately, it is often unnecessary, unproductive urgency at play. It is an urgency that increases activity levels and stress levels, but does not necessarily increase results. And this urgency can be so prevalent that we no longer see it or recognise it when it takes over.

Think about the emails you receive with URGENT[10] boldly typed in the subject line that are not urgent at all. Or the meetings that get called at a moment's notice to discuss things that really could have waited. Or even an interruption from a colleague just because they caught your eye when you were on your way to a meeting.

Urgency mainly arises from personal workstyles, behaviours and expectations, not from the type of industry or organisation you work within. If you look close enough you will begin to notice the signs of unnecessary urgency all around you.

But don't get me wrong. Urgency is not inherently a bad thing and, in fact, many leaders and managers would say that a sense of urgency is critical to create traction and momentum with important projects in their organisations. This is what I call *productive urgency*.

However, much of what we call 'urgent' is harmful to our productivity and our wellbeing. Many urgent things are unnecessarily urgent or are not even pressing at all — they are masquerading as urgent and creating stress and distracting us from more important work. This is what I call *unproductive urgency*.

---

[10] It has been amusing to receive many emails recently with URGENT! in the subject line, get mildly upset with the sender, then realise that it is my book title they where referring to.

At the individual level we create this when we procrastinate, fail to plan properly and adopt reactive workstyles. At the team level unproductive urgency is created when managers don't protect their team by negotiating and pushing back on urgency. And at the organisational level unproductive urgency is created when leaders permit a culture of urgency to exist. Or worse, when leaders drive a culture of urgency!

Sometimes, rather than creating a *sense* of urgency we are creating *senseless* urgency.

Over the years I have worked with many organisations where urgency and reactivity are the norm. As a trainer and a consultant, I get to peek behind the curtain and see what is really happening. Many of the people in these organisations don't see the problem — they are too close to it. They are living it. But as an outsider I can tell when there is a reactive culture, and I can see the behaviours that lead to people working in the reactive zone for too long. And I desperately want to help, because I passionately believe that we don't have to work in a constant state of urgency and reactivity. I believe that if we slowed down a bit, we would actually get more work done, and better quality work at that.

Urgency is a very necessary tool to getting things done, but must be used with the following in mind. It must be:

- used purposefully

- used sparingly

- moderated so that it stays within acceptable limits.

Yet most of us have come to expect urgency as the normal rough and tumble of business, and we become victims of it.

We feel powerless to change it, and just accept urgent requests, meetings and email responses as a part of our day. We fall into the trap of thinking that urgency is just the way it is. But if we give in to urgency, we pay a real cost.

As we will explore further on, chronic and acute urgency causes unnecessary stress, friction and burnout. It also gets in the way of the important work that might not be urgent, but can provide huge value if we can make time for it. Worst of all, unfettered urgency shapes the culture of an organisation, creating toxic environments that sap morale and wellbeing.

Remember, industries are not reactive by nature. Organisations are not reactive by nature. It is individuals who cause reactivity and urgency most of the time.

Reactivity is a choice we make when faced with urgency. And our choices become our actions.

CHAPTER 1

What is urgency and why does it matter?

Urgency sure is a funny beast. It is not a physical thing, yet it shapes how we work. It is not a feeling yet it can make us feel stressed and out of control. It is not a school of thought, yet it can become a mindset, and it can cause devastation if not controlled. In the words of author Jonathan Lockwood Huie, 'Time is carnivorous. Urgency rips the peaceful flesh from our bones.'

The word 'urgent' comes from the Latin 'urgentum', which means to press hard or urge. The word 'urge' itself means to demand or insist. It is a word that has become embedded in our corporate vocabulary, but in many ways has lost its true meaning for many of us.

The Oxford Dictionary defines urgency as

'importance requiring swift action'.

There are many variations on this in other dictionaries, but I like the simplicity of this one. You may have noticed that the word is used in a much looser way in our workplaces, and we often don't fully honour that definition.

If 'urgent' was truly kept for occasions where the issue was important and needing swift action, I would not be writing this book! But the truth is we use 'urgent' to describe anything that is slightly time critical, whether it's important or not. And of course, importance is so subjective. What is important to me might not be important to you.

So, for the purposes of this book I will define urgency as anything that requires swift action, important or not. While I would like you to only be dealing with urgent issues that are a good use of your time, the reality is you are dealing with all types of urgency. There will be things that are both important and urgent. There will be things that are only urgent, and even things that are not at all urgent, but somebody is kicking up a fuss. We need to deal with it all.

What is it that makes something urgent? How do you spot it? Usually it's the proximity to a deadline, so it is mostly time-related. But urgency can also be driven by inaction; i.e. it's the consequence of not acting on something. And urgency can also be driven by insistence. Think about the noise your fridge makes when you leave the door open — it is designed to drive you nuts so you close it quickly! Many things communicate urgency to us, and many types of people that we work with can create it ...

The eight faces of urgency

In chapter 2 we explore the different types of urgency in detail. In the meantime, let's have a look at why and how urgency might show up in our workplace. There are many reasons why urgency occurs, but much of the time it is down to our personal behaviours. And over time these behaviours become habits that influence how we work.

The eight characters listed here represent the typical people who create urgency and reactivity in their work. See if you recognise any of them.

The Reactor[11]

Joanne—marketing assistant in a national retail company

Joanne works hard. She is young and keen to get ahead. She prides herself on the long hours she is willing to work and on her quick responses to any request or query. Unfortunately, even with the long hours she puts in, she is struggling to stay on top of everything. Her inbox is overflowing with emails and she feels constantly behind in her work. She tries to stay on top of the never-ending flow of requests but feels that she is just jumping from one urgent issue to another.

Joanne usually reacts to emails the minute they come in and tries to move them on, but because of this constant distraction, she then falls behind on her other priorities. She ends up reacting to these priorities when they, in turn, become urgent. Her stress levels are at an all-time high, and the quality of her work is beginning to slip. She worries that her performance meeting with her manager next week is not going to go so well.

The Conductor

Claude—executive manager in a large bank

Managing a team is not easy, especially in an organisation as large and complex as Claude's. He tries hard to keep his eight

---

[11] No workers were harmed in the writing of this book, and all names and characters are fictitious.

direct reports focused and on track. But they get so much pressure from the other parts of the organisation they support. Everyone seems to think his team have unlimited resources at their disposal. Many think their issue should be the number one priority for his team, and they all want it ASAP. But what can he do? That is the role.

Claude feels his reputation depends on the ability of his team to deliver, so he tries hard to meet the demands of the other units. He knows that he should probably push back more, but his boss sees him as someone who gets things done. Rather than pushing back on the tight deadlines that end up in the laps of his already overwhelmed team, he desperately tries to juggle their workload and to squeeze a bit more out of them. Deep down, though, he worries. He knows this cannot last, and that people will start to leave if nothing changes. In fact, he is considering moving on himself to something a little less pressured.

The Over-Committer
Kyle—partner in a top-tier consulting firm

'Give me a deadline and I will smash it!' That is Kyle's motto, and he lives and breathes it. He does not believe in planning systems or inbox management strategies. He just does what needs to be done and drives his team to do the same. Of course, he plans and prioritises in his head, and always has his most urgent priorities top of mind.

Kyle likes to go above and beyond for clients. He manages a couple of large corporate accounts that provide good revenue for his firm. So, if they want to meet with him, he clears his schedule and makes it happen that day. And if they need a report, he promises it will be on their desk first thing the next morning. He then enlists his team to help, who often have to clear their schedules or their evening plans to get it done. Nothing is too much trouble for Kyle, and he always believes that nothing should be too much trouble for his team either. Unbeknownst to Kyle, his team feel resentful that they often have to scramble to deliver something to a client in an urgent way, when the client probably does not need it that quickly in the first place. The pressure created for them is immense and, they feel, often unnecessary.

The Last-Minute Delegator

Julie—operations manager in a not-for-profit health services provider

Julie is passionate about her job and the outcomes she achieves for her clients. It is important work. Unfortunately, she has never been very organised and struggles to manage her time and priorities, especially now that she is receiving so many emails every day. She tries to stay on top of her inbox, but it is a struggle. Things often slip through the cracks and she is regularly chased by other people for responses and actions.

She knows that one of her worst habits is being indecisive with emails that contain actions which should be delegated to others. Her normal behaviour is to look at the email, but if it is not screamingly urgent, leave it in her inbox until later. She then delegates the work when she is being chased for it, rather than when she recieves it. This puts a lot of pressure on her team, as she is usually delegating at the last minute. She feels bad, but it's just so hard to keep up with everything!

The Distractor

Alistair—Australian CEO of a midsize multinational tech company

Since stepping into the CEO role last year, Alistair has been focused on growth and revenue. The strategic plan is clear in his head, and the board seem happy with progress. He's an ideas man with great energy and drive. He is a good leader and inspires and motivates his team to achieve great things.

They have an activity-based workplace and he likes to work in the open plan space with the team, even though he has his own office as well. That way he can be where the action is and be seen to be one of the team. He often walks the floor, touching base with key team members, sharing his thoughts and checking in on progress and issues. This is commendable but has a negative side effect.

What Alistair does not realise is that his habit of throwing ideas at his team whenever he thinks of them is creating a lot of unnecessary work. What is just an offhand comment or thought bubble for him feels more like a directive to them, and they often jump onto it and action it right away. Unfortunately, by the time they deliver a draft to him, he has moved on and forgotten about it. These drafts pile up on his desk, never seeing the light of day again. His unfocused habit of thinking out loud is distracting his team from more important priorities.

The Hard Driver

Anne—senior marketing director in a multinational insurance company

Anne has a very busy role, managing a large marketing team and working with different parts of the local business, as well as reporting to both the US and Asian regional offices. She is very experienced in the role, and drives her team hard, but feels she is a fair boss—hard but fair.

She personally has always just got things done. She would work long hours to deliver what was required and expects her people to do the same. Over the past couple of years, the pressure has increased, with some large projects to be delivered, and lots of day-to-day issues to be resolved. All of this is happening in the midst of a global restructure. Things have always been busy for her and the team, but she has not seen that they are now operating in a constant state of reactivity. There is always a crisis to be managed, and this has become the norm.

She forges ahead doing what she has always done, pushing through as hard as possible. But she piles new priorities on top of old priorities, increasing people's workloads to impossible levels. She sees her team struggling to stay on top of things, and to be honest, she is beginning to struggle herself. She can tell that something is not right but cannot seem to define the problem or the solution.

The Procrastinator

Jing—financial analyst in a manufacturing company

Jing is keen to make an impression with her new boss. She knows that if she works hard there is a promotion opportunity in the next few months. Her work involves some in-depth analysis balanced with a lot of day-to-day requests. While she knows that the deep analysis work is important, and what she really gets measured on, her preference is to clear the day-to-day stuff before getting stuck into the more complex work.

But there are so many requests that she often gets caught up in dealing with these, leaving the other more important work for later. Eventually the important priorities catch up with her, and she cannot put them off any longer. She then finds herself under pressure and has recently made a few mistakes that have not gone unnoticed. She feels that she is doing her best and doing what is asked. What more can she do?

The Boy Who Cried Wolf
Peter—salesperson in a tech company

Peter is a great salesperson who hits his targets without fail. To make sure he keeps his clients happy, he often places orders on their behalf and tells head office that the orders are extremely urgent, even if they are not. His customers love the fast service, but the office staff are sick of the constant pressure he creates. They know his orders are not that urgent, and they are getting close to ignoring them in favour of other salespeople who are more respectful. Maybe he has cried wolf once too often!

————

The characters detailed above are not real, but you may recognise them because they demonstrate behaviours that we see every day in our workplaces. They are our bosses, our teammates, our leaders.

One of them may well be you.

For the most part they have good intentions. But their behaviours, habits and workstyles cause reactivity and urgency all too often. And they cause the worst form of urgency—unproductive urgency. This is a big problem that affects the productivity and wellbeing of everyone involved.

The cost of urgency

So, what is the real problem here? You may feel that there are few downsides to urgency, just upsides. What's wrong with getting more done, faster? Surely that's the best way to achieve what we need to, make more sales, deliver better service and generate more profits for our businesses?

Not necessarily.

It is possible that we've become so accustomed to the fast pace of business and the constant deadlines that we don't actually recognise the cost of urgency, so it's important we look at that now. Here are some ways that urgency and reactivity work *against* us.

Inefficient use of time and resources

Unnecessary urgency makes us very busy. Whether urgency is pressed upon us or self-inflicted, it creates a pattern of activity that can be described as 'chasing our tails' or 'running around like headless chickens'. We end up jumping from one urgent issue to another, feeling incredibly busy and stretched, yet not being truly effective in our work. And the fact that we are reacting to issues rather than working proactively increases the chances that mistakes will be made, which leads to missed opportunities and wasted time.

At the individual level this is bad, but if you have a whole team that works reactively the problem grows infinitely worse.

A few years ago, working with the publishing department in a retail company I saw a lot of time being wasted due to the amount of urgency that people had to deal with. The department produced the brochures that advertised the retail group's products and special offers. There were strict deadlines that needed to be met, but even though this was their everyday work, there was an obvious lack of planning. Everyone was overworked and overwhelmed, and often left things until the last minute. This meant they were constantly being chased by others to get the work in before deadlines were missed.

There was a lot of wasted time and resources in this team, but most of it was self-inflicted and unnecessary. It should not be this hard. As a business they needed to not only train staff on how to manage their work more proactively, but also to look in the mirror and examine how they had created a culture that promoted and rewarded urgency. To their credit they worked on this and created a more effective workplace.

Avoidable rework

Rework is a hidden but very real cost to businesses. In manufacturing organisations, a lot of effort goes into reducing wastage and rework in the manufacturing process. If a part is not manufactured correctly the first time, there is a very measurable cost to the bottom line for that product. So, factories will have systems and processes in place to reduce the error rate. In fact, this will be one of the key stats that is measured daily. The efficiency of the manufacturing process is measured constantly to maximise productivity and profitability.

But unlike in manufacturing, knowledge work organisations may not see the wastage, downtime and rework that is created because of unnecessary urgency.

Too much reactivity can lead to avoidable mistakes, wasting time and resources on redoing work.

We will avoid a lot of rework if we just slow down a bit and do it right the first time.

An increase in stress levels

In their white paper 'A Theory of Workplace Anxiety', Bonnie Hayden Cheng and Julie McCarthy cite research that indicates 40 per cent of Americans report feeling anxious during their workday, and 72 per cent of these people feel that this anxiety affects their work and personal lives.

Now of course there are many factors that might contribute to workplace anxiety, including cranky bosses, unhelpful colleagues or unrealistic workloads. But urgency is definitely a major factor as well.

Increased anxiety is bound to affect performance and wellbeing. We do not think as clearly when we are anxious, we don't feel as motivated, and sometimes we just opt out because of it.

The funny thing is, some people actively create urgent situations because they thrive on the stress of a deadline. Sometimes we leave things until the deadline, telling ourselves the story that we do our best work at the last minute. We convince ourselves that we need the pressure of a deadline to perform, especially with creative or complex work.

I reckon this is a story that began at school and at university. We would leave assignments and studying for exams until the last minute and then would have to cram the night before.[12]

Surely there is enough stress in our roles already without creating more unnecessarily.

---

[12] Or was that just me? I remember many nights staring at a page hours before an exam, convincing myself that it was a stupid exam anyway, but knowing deep down that I should have started studying earlier. Much earlier!

A drop in quality

Whether we are reacting blindly to incoming urgency, or leaving things until the last minute ourselves, the quality of our work suffers. We make mistakes because we rush things. We compromise the finished product because we run out of time. And in the knowledge workplace, we lose the time to stop and think.

A recent KPMG Global CEO survey found that 86 per cent of global leaders struggled to find time to think about two of the most critical drivers in their businesses: disruption and innovation. In Australia that percentage crept up to 94 per cent. When you think about the role a leader plays in steering the organisation in the right direction, and navigating the challenges in a complex and volatile environment, not having enough time to think is very problematic.

I am not surprised by this, though. This issue comes up every time I work with a leadership team on their productivity. They are so pressured during the day with meetings, emails and interruptions, they have no time to really think, make sense of things, connect the dots or make quality decisions.

This drop in quality happens at all levels in organisations, and can have quite a dramatic impact. One day, when I was running a personal productivity workshop for a medical research company, I was told of an urgency issue that could possibly have life or death ramifications. They were a medical research organisation and worked closely with many of the top pharmaceutical companies around the world. One of the key issues they faced was email overload, with some of the team receiving hundreds of emails every day. Many of these emails would claim to be urgent.

When I suggested they take a more proactive approach to email by turning off their email alerts, there was uproar in the room! Now, I'm used to this: most people are addicted to the little dopamine hit we get when we hear the little email alert go 'bing'. The debate and conversation that followed was fascinating. Some were all for turning their email alerts off, saying it was ridiculous that they were so beholden to their inboxes. Others argued that they would like to, but felt the expectation was that they would always respond to emails within a few minutes.

Then one senior manager voiced her thoughts. She said that some of the emails they received were actually about life-threatening situations in hospital theatres, where the surgeons needed critical information about medication from the pharma company, and the pharma company in turn needed to discuss this with the research team.

The challenge she framed, though, was that although these emails were truly urgent, they were being drowned out by all the other 'business as usual' emails that were labelled as urgent as well. When *everything* is urgent, guess what? Then *nothing* is really urgent.

Burnout and attrition

This is the big one for me. If urgency becomes the norm in a team or an organisation, it becomes a part of the culture. While organisations may be able to operate through periods of high reactivity in short bursts, if working in the reactive zone becomes a long-term part of the culture, then burnout and attrition will surely follow.

People might not be able to name it as a reason, but they will have a feeling that has built up over time: feelings of increased stress, agitation and frustration. They might not mention chronic urgency as an issue, but they may say that they can no longer cope with the hectic pace. They might suggest that they would prefer a role that gave them more control over their work. They may frame their disquiet in terms of yearning for more balance, or a role that has more meaning. All of these issues could be caused by many factors, but too much urgency is in each of them to a degree.

I believe that most people want to do meaningful work that makes a difference. But working in reactive cultures can feel like constantly walking into a headwind. It is hard work.

And after a while on the urgency treadmill, we lose our motivation and move on to something easier.

Whether we find it in our next role, who knows, but some organisations are better at managing this than others. Chronic urgency is one of the factors that contributes to a toxic culture in organisations. And urgency can become contagious. As more and more people work reactively, this way of working spreads and becomes normal. Once a culture has become toxic, it takes a lot of work to change. Over time, people will leave to find roles in organisations that are less toxic and easier to work in.

If you are a manager or a leader, do you want to lose good people because of this? I doubt it. You put a lot of effort into training them up, and the reality is that their leaving is probably going to make things even more reactive for you in the short term.

A compelling case for change

I have the pleasure of working in many different organisations around the world. I get to work closely with leadership, managers and workers in banks, consulting firms, hospitals, insurance companies, retail giants, law firms, manufacturing organisations, sales and marketing companies and funeral homes. A very diverse range of industries, you would agree. But in most cases, I am walking into cultures and teams that feel under unnecessary pressure because of the constant urgency they face.

Now is the time to make a change. Now is the perfect time to learn to manage urgency and to develop a more proactive way of working.

Whether you are a worker, a manager or a leader, you have a role to play in moderating the urgency in your workplace. You have some power and agency in this regard, and there are things you can do to manage it. Let's explore urgency in all its glorious forms and develop some strategies to leverage this force for good, not evil. Let's be quick, we have no time to waste![13]

---

[13] There I go again!

URGENCY PLAYBOOK
PRINCIPLE 1

DON'T CRY WOLF

Don't make work out to be urgent if it's not, or more urgent than it needs to be. Save urgency for when it is unavoidable, important and truly time critical.

The old tale about the boy who cried wolf teaches a lesson that is still relevant today. He cried wolf too many times when there was no danger of a wolf attacking the village. Then the day came when there really was a wolf, and no-one believed him when he raised the alarm.

If I recall correctly, I believe he was eaten by the wolf! So, the lesson here is don't cry 'Urgent' unless it truly is, lest you are devoured by your colleagues!

When I run our personal productivity workshop, there is a lot of focus on email management. One of the things that constantly surprises me is the amount of email people get where the subject line starts with the word 'urgent'. But that is just level 1. Level 2 is 'URGENT!' Level 3 is 'REALLY URGENT!' And on it goes, with people trying to jostle to the front of our attention in our crowded inboxes.

While I understand this partially happens because most people do not manage their inboxes well—they are overwhelmed by the deluge of constant emails, so others need to deploy urgency in order to be seen—I also feel that sometimes the sender of these emails may have a reactive mindset, and therefore makes everything more urgent than it needs to be.

I sometimes dream of an urgency token system: you get five tokens at the start of each month, and you have to use a token every time you create urgency for someone else. When you run out of tokens, that's it for the month! Of course, I'm not being serious, but imagine how our mindsets would change if we had limits placed on our ability to create urgency!

CHAPTER 2

Productive versus unproductive urgency

I reckon urgency is a bit like ice cream. It's so easy to eat and becomes a bit addictive for many of us. We convince ourselves we don't actually eat that much ice cream, yet find ourselves eating it every time we pass the fridge or open the menu. Like ice cream, urgent issues:

- are a welcome distraction from the mundane

- make us feel good

- have so many flavours to choose from!

Here are some of the flavours of urgency that tempt us daily:

- There is the good urgency that leads to better results with our work; and there is the bad, which just creates stress and confusion, and in fact wastes more time in the long run.

- Some urgency is real and must be addressed quickly; and some urgency is fake, when we or someone else makes something urgent when it is not.

- Some is avoidable and some unavoidable.

- Some urgency is self-inflicted and some is pressed upon us by others.

- Finally, there is productive urgency and there is unproductive urgency.

Who would have thought! All of these different flavours of urgency in your workplace, driving your busy-ness and ruining your appetite for dinner.[14]

But it's confusing to be on the lookout for so many types of urgency, so the key differentiation we will explore here is between *productive* and *unproductive* urgency, and the causes of each.

When we understand something, we can deal with it more intelligently. Figure 2.1 creates a simple framework to understand urgency and how it is caused.

Fake urgency

Sometimes things seem urgent, but actually are not. I believe many urgent requests in our workplaces fall under this category. How often have you reacted to an email alert, replying immediately even though it was not actually urgent, and certainly not as important as the work you were trying to concentrate on beforehand? That was you making something

---

[14] Dinner being your important priorities. I know, sometimes I flog an analogy too hard!

			PRODUCTIVE
REASONABLE URGENCY	Others	6. Someone else identified an issue/opportunity and passed it to you	
	You	5. You identified an issue/opportunity that requires swift action	
AVOIDABLE URGENCY	Others	4. Someone else left it until the last minute, then passed it to you	UNPRODUCTIVE
	You	3. You left it until the last minute and created problems for yourself	
FAKE URGENCY	Others	2. Someone else made it seem urgent, even though it was not	
	You	1. You made it seem urgent yourself, even though it was not	

Figure 2.1: productive vs unproductive urgency

urgent even though it was not, and dealing with it in what I call 'the first minute'. It is self-inflicted urgency, when you are actually your own worst enemy.

Now think about the times someone else landed an 'urgent' issue on your plate that you absolutely knew was not urgent; it's just that they have worked out that if they scream loud enough, they get what they want.[15]

Both of those examples are *fake urgency* showing up to derail your day. Fake urgency is very common, and has a number of root causes:

- other people having unreasonable expectations of us
- us making things urgent for ourselves and not clarifying expectations
- a lack of communication and clarity around deadlines
- our own addiction to urgency.

Avoidable urgency

Next comes urgency that is real but could have been avoided but was not. This type of urgency must be the most prolific in today's workplace and may also be the most disruptive. How often have you left a piece of work until the last minute, even though you knew you had a looming deadline? This is procrastination—a very human failing. You may recall the Procrastinator from chapter 1, one of the eight faces of urgency. We are all busy and procrastinate sometimes, but unfortunately it happens too often for comfort.

---

[15] Do you recognise some of these behaviours in the eight characters in chapter 1?

Even worse, what about when other people leave it until the last minute, and then hand the urgency over to you? There is a saying that goes something like 'a lack of planning on your part should not cause a crisis for me'. Whether it was caused by yourself or someone else, this type of urgency is avoidable and should be minimised as much as possible.

Some root causes of avoidable urgency are:

- reactive cultures
- last-minute workstyles and mindsets
- procrastination
- disorganisation
- over-promising and under delivering
- poor estimation of task duration.

Both fake and avoidable urgency are unproductive. They needlessly slow us down and stress us out.

Reasonable urgency

Lastly, there are the things that are urgent, and could not have been planned for. In these scenarios we identify an issue or opportunity that requires swift action.

Sometimes others come to us with work that is unavoidably urgent, and it is totally appropriate that we respond as needed.

This is life, and as long as you are comfortable that it is a good use of your time, it is your job.

This is *productive urgency*. If you think about it, this is really the only type of urgency we should accept. And it should be a rare occurrence, not an everyday one. Maybe 10 to 20 per cent of our time should be spent dealing with this type of urgent work. If we could reduce false and avoidable urgency, we would have a lot more time spent working proactively. And guess what? The more proactively we work, the less reactive we will become in the future. It becomes a virtuous cycle of proactivity. And that is good for us, our team and our organisation.

What are the root causes of this reasonable urgency?

- unplannable scenarios[16]

- unexpected opportunities

- unforeseen issues.

Ideally, we would want to avoid this type of urgency as well, but that may prove impossible. We need to ensure we are in a position to deal with this urgency when it does arise. A valid part of any job or role is dealing with unforeseen issues, and you will never plan for everything. But it is also important to spot and leverage opportunities when they come your way, and we need to ensure that we are on our toes and ready to respond when they do.

We need to minimise unproductive urgency and position ourselves to deal with productive urgency appropriately.

---

[16] Who could have foreseen COVID-19 and all of its consequences for businesses around the world?

How to spot unproductive urgency

I am very lucky to be surrounded by some very cool friends and colleagues, many of them leading experts in their fields. Or as we say in Ireland, they are like a Kerry farmer — outstanding in their field![17] One of these clever people is my friend Stacey Barr,[18] a performance measurement expert and author of *Prove It!* and *Practical Performance Measurement*. Stacey is also the creator of the PuMP measurement system, which is used in organisations around the world to create more relevant and tangible measures for performance.

I asked Stacey if workplace urgency was measurable. Her response was 'Let's find out!' Stacey walked me through a clarification exercise that is a part of the PuMP methodology, which was extremely enlightening. The end result was that yes, workplace urgency definitely is measurable, and is worth measuring.

One of the questions that Stacey asked me was, 'If you walked into an organisation that was very reactive and driven by urgency, what would you notice? How would the urgency show itself?' This simple question got me thinking. How urgency shows up is a bit like what they call a 'tell' in poker: an unconscious movement, tic or behaviour that gives away the player's strategy or thinking. If you look around you, you will see lots of 'tells' if urgency is showing up every day. Once you become aware of urgency, especially unnecessary negative urgency, you will become intolerant of it, because it has such a negative impact on your productivity and the productivity of your team.

---

[17] My editor struggled to get this one, so I had better explain my Irish humour. An Irish farmer spends a lot of time standing in fields. Outstanding in his field — get it?

[18] Learn more about her here: www.staceybarr.com

A good way to think about how urgency shows up in your workplace is to think about whether the urgency is a 'first minute' behaviour, or a 'last minute' behaviour.

What are the 'tells' that we are being forced to react and work in the first minute? One obvious tell would be that you and your team have email alerts turned on, and always seem to be looking at your phones in meetings.

What are the 'tells' that we are reacting to work at the last minute? Maybe you seem to be up against last-minute deadlines a bit too often for comfort. If we can identify what is causing this reactivity we can manage it.

Now overlay this with the idea that some urgency is pressed on us by others, and some urgency is self-inflicted.

First-minute, pressed upon us

These intrusions into our carefully planned day force us to react and can have a real impact on our other priorities. Research reckons that even a momentary interruption can take us up to 20 minutes to recover from, as we attempt to refocus on what we were doing before.

Sometimes these intrusions are for truly urgent issues, and if so, we should prioritise them over less urgent work and deal with them in a timely way. They represent productive urgency. But if they are pressed upon us by others and they are not really urgent, they just distract us from what's really important. Examples of this might be:

- unnecessary interruptions
- last-minute requests
- last-minute work delegations

- unrealistic deadlines

- emails with 'urgent' in the subject line

- meetings called at short notice

- working in a culture of urgency.

Last-minute, pressed upon us

In this scenario, other people's last-minute reactive behaviours have an impact on our productivity. When other people leave things until the last minute and then pass the urgency on to us, it can also have a negative impact on our productivity. Sometimes the issue here is environmental, such as too much work or too few resources.

The challenge here is that everyone is busy and doing their best to get everything done. But some people are more organised than others, are better at prioritising, and may also be better at negotiating their workloads. The ones who are not are the ones that cause us most problems in this quadrant. Some examples might be:

- we need to chase others for responses

- meetings are cancelled same day

- urgent requests for information

- too much work on our plate

- too few resources in team

- workflow bottlenecks

- constantly changing priorities.

Self-inflicted, first-minute

This problem is of our own making. If our own workstyle is reactive, we can find ourselves mindlessly reacting to non-critical inputs. We often do this because of the need to please others or to feel in control of what is happening. But this way of working increases stress levels and reduces the quality of our focus and our work.

This issue has become more challenging in the modern workplace with so much mobile technology at our fingertips. It is too easy to get sucked into a reactive way of working when we are so accessible. Examples of this are:

- reacting to email alerts

- constantly checking phones

- being distracted in meetings

- engaging in people-pleasing behaviours

- not negotiating deadlines

- assuming urgency

- reacting to positions of authority.

Self-inflicted, last-minute

The final quadrant describes things that, again, are our own fault as we only make time for them when they are close to (or past) their deadline. The problem here is often related to the systems we use to organise ourselves. In my experience most people use priority and task management systems that are more geared towards reactivity rather than proactivity. We examine this further in chapter 4.

When we leave things until the last minute, we force ourselves into a position of having to react to something that could have been done at an earlier time. Again, stress levels rise, and the quality of the work goes down. Examples are:

- work left until the last minute

- overdue task lists

- others need to chase us

- frequent procrastination

- projects put off until later

- missed deadlines

- late to meetings.

————

Have a think about your own personal workstyle. Can you see any signs of unproductive urgency?

Now think about your team. Do you see any signs in how they work? Zoom out to your organisation. Do you see this happening at a cultural level? The first step to fixing a problem is to recognise that it is happening and to name it. The next step is to understand if the issue is caused by personal workstyle, by the environment, or by both.

How reactive are you?

So, we have established that unproductive urgency is a bad thing—no arguments there, I hope. But knowing that is one thing; *doing* something about it is another. How can we actually change our ingrained habits and behaviours, and how do we influence the reactive culture that we might work within?

The best starting point is to get a feel for how reactive or proactive your personal workstyle might be. And while we're at it, why don't we get a feel for how you perceive your environment: is it chaotic or ordered?

Have a look at the questions in the following questionnaire (see figure 2.2). There are eight questions related to personal workstyle and eight questions related to your environment. Circle where you feel you sit in each scale. Go with your gut instinct, but be honest with yourself. If you aren't going to be honest, stop reading this and go and do something more urgent instead![19]

---

[19] Please don't—but you know what I'm saying.

PERSONAL WORKSTYLE

1. I react to email alerts on my phone and computer.

2. I leave tasks and priorities until the last minute.

3. I interrupt others with urgent requests and delegations.

4. I underestimate how much time complex tasks require to be completed.

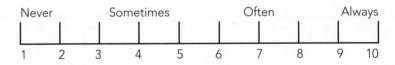

Figure 2.2: reactive/proactive questionnaire

PERSONAL WORKSTYLE (cont'd)

5. I make mistakes in my work which leads to rework.

Never		Sometimes				Often		Always	
1	2	3	4	5	6	7	8	9	10

6. I like the thrill of deadlines.

Never		Sometimes				Often		Always	
1	2	3	4	5	6	7	8	9	10

7. Others need to chase me for work and information.

Never		Sometimes				Often		Always	
1	2	3	4	5	6	7	8	9	10

8. I procrastinate important but less urgent activities.

Never		Sometimes				Often		Always	
1	2	3	4	5	6	7	8	9	10

Figure 2.2: reactive/proactive questionnaire (*cont'd*)

WORK ENVIRONMENT

1. My plan for the day is thrown out the window due to urgent issues that crop up.

2. I feel I have no control over the reactivity of my workplace.

3. I am pulled into meetings at short notice.

4. Reacting quickly to emails and messages is expected and rewarded in my workplace.

Figure 2.2: reactive/proactive questionnaire (*cont'd*)

WORK ENVIRONMENT (cont'd)

5. I need to chase others for expected work and information.

6. Planned meetings are cancelled at the last minute.

7. Priorities and directives from above change and shift.

```
Never          Sometimes              Often          Always
|    |    |    |    |    |    |    |    |    |
1    2    3    4    5    6    7    8    9    10
```

8. My team and colleagues seem stressed and under pressure.

```
Never          Sometimes              Often          Always
|    |    |    |    |    |    |    |    |    |
1    2    3    4    5    6    7    8    9    10
```

Figure 2.2: reactive/proactive questionnaire (*cont'd*)

Total up your scores for your personal workstyle questions. You should end up with a score out of 80, such as 52/80. Do the same for your work environment questions. This should give you two scores to work with.

Your personal workstyle score is: _____

If you scored more than 40 for personal workstyle, you will be on the left-hand side of the dividing line in the matrix on page 38. This suggests you may have a *reactive workstyle*. If you scored less than 40 for personal workstyle, you will be on the right-hand side of the dividing line in the matrix. This suggests you may have a *proactive workstyle*.

Your work environment score is: _____

If you scored more than 40 for work environment, you will be below the dividing line in the matrix. This suggests you may work in a *chaotic environment*. If you scored less than 40 for work environment, you will be above the dividing line in the matrix. This suggests you work in an *ordered workplace*.

You should find yourself placed in one of the four quadrants:

1. **Frenzied.** Workstyle score more than 40; environment score more than 40.

2. **Disruptive.** Workstyle score more than 40; environment score less than 40.

3. **Disrupted.** Workstyle score less than 40; environment score more than 40.

4. **Productive.** Workstyle score less than 40; environment score less than 40.

These quadrants are illustrated on figure 2.3 (overleaf).

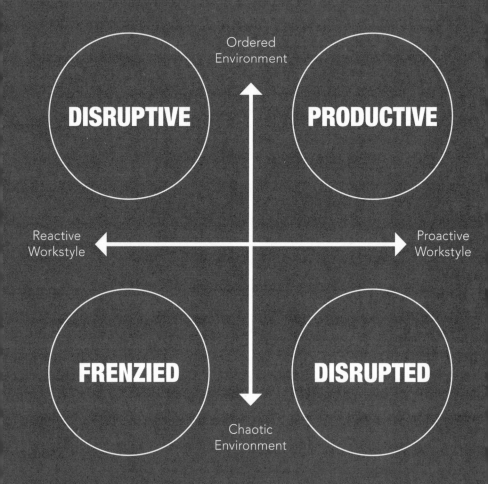

Figure 2.3: workstyle/environment matrix

1. Frenzied

Workstyle score more than 40;
environment score more than 40

If you find yourself in this quadrant, your personal workstyle is reactive, and your environment is also quite chaotic. Of course, the two are connected, so this may not come as a surprise. This may be killing you, or you may feel like you thrive in this zone, and may have gravitated to an organisation or a team like this because you like the energy.

You are like a kid in a candy store, revelling in the freedom to leave things until the last minute just like everyone else does.

And not only do you love working this way, but your team may love it too, because it fits with their worldview. This is why the culture and the environment feel reactive and chaotic. In the long run this is not a productive quadrant to work in, and it has long-term consequences for you and those around you.

Stress levels and burnout are high here; it's hard to keep up the pace of reactivity. There is the potential for a lot of mistakes to be made and rework needed in this quadrant, which you may dismiss or justify as just the cost of getting a lot done.

As a consultant, I personally find it very challenging to work with teams like this, full of reactive people in a reactive environment. I can only imagine what it's like to work in these teams long term. It is certainly the choice of some, but I suspect that many leave or move on as they struggle to deal with the chaos.

There are lots of strategies that can be applied to help you and your team to dial down the urgency and work more proactively.

Pay special attention to the strategies outlined in part II on minimising personal reactivity. But you should also think about your environment and have a discussion about whether all this urgency is really needed. As a team you could create a more proactive culture that gets better results.

2. Disruptive

Workstyle score more than 40;
environment score less than 40

If you are in this quadrant, your workstyle reactivity is high, but the environment around you is more ordered. So you may be working against the flow, causing disruption for those around you. Your colleagues may get frustrated by the urgent pressure you put on their plate because of your reactivity and lack of organisation.

> ## You're like a bull in a china shop, wreaking havoc on everything and everyone around you with your reactive, urgent ways.

You may justify this by thinking that everyone has their own way of working and that the workplace needs to be flexible. But effective team players aim to be productive for themselves and for those around them.[20] The productivity friction you create for others makes it hard for them to focus on their priorities and may stop them from doing their best work.

It breaks my heart when I see managers who are like this. They often don't realise the negative impact they have on their teams, and don't recognise there could be a better and easier way of working.

---

[20] I explore this idea more fully in my book *Smart Teams.*

If this is you, think hard about how your behaviours affect others, and consider talking to your teammates about their experience with this. If yours is a primarily proactive team, they will have strategies to share with you that may help you to help them.

3. Disrupted

Workstyle score less than 40;
environment score more than 40

If your preference is to work proactively, but you are working in a highly reactive team or organisation, this can be really hard. Your attempts to work productively are limited, and you can get frustrated at the constant urgency and reactivity. Your best efforts to work in a proactive way are disrupted by others' lack of planning. You constantly get dragged into urgent meetings, are delegated work at the last minute, and always seem to be pulled this way and that, no matter how much you plan. (Argh! ...)

You are like a square peg in a round hole, constantly working against a culture that does not support your way of working.

I often come across people in this situation. One day I ran a follow-up training session for a busy operations team in a large bank. They had completed my Smart Work training a couple of months before, and I had offered to come back and work with them for an hour on any implementation issues.

The group were very positive about their progress and the benefits they were seeing from the initial training, but as we talked a couple of issues came up. One was the meeting culture in their area. They were in constant meetings, many of them last minute and urgent, and had very little time left over to get any of their other priorities completed during normal working hours.

The second issue was the volume of urgent issues that came their way every day—what they called 'escalations'—that ate into any proactive time they did have. It was all very well getting their inbox down to zero, and centralising their tasks into MS Outlook, but if they had no time to get any of this stuff done, what was the point?

They felt frustrated as they were trying to implement an effective personal productivity system, but were being derailed by a culture that was reactive and driven by urgency. This scenario is what we often call 'firefighting': constantly putting out (metaphorical) fires and then jumping from one fire to another. It is not a good way to work. One of the managers in the group admitted that he had been working in operations roles for years, but had never experienced this level of reactivity in other organisations.

When your environment is reactive, you need to work hard to create a cultural shift.

And this is not easy, especially if you are not the person in authority. Rather than using positional authority, you will need to build informal authority strategies that can influence those around you. Team agreements around how priorities and deadlines are managed are critical, and some team training in personal productivity would be helpful for the team. If everyone commits to a common system for managing their time, priorities and emails, it can have a dramatic impact on the reactivity of a team. But even just raising awareness and talking about it as a team can be helpful. Just don't be a victim and feel that you have no control here.

4. Productive

Workstyle score less than 40;
environment score less than 40

This final quadrant is the one you would ideally like to see yourself in. Here you have a proactive workstyle and you work within a predominantly proactive environment. This is good. Productive work can get done here in a timely way, with less stress and burnout. That does not mean there is a complete absence of urgent issues or behaviours, but they are the exception rather than the rule.

There's not too much to improve here, except to check in with your team on their views. Do they also see your workstyle as proactive, and their environment as proactive? If not, you may have a warped sense of what's happening!

But hopefully, they'll agree. So, if they do, then keep doing what you're doing: work productively and achieve great things without creating too much drama. You have a good approach to work and are working in an environment that supports and appreciates it.

You are like a productive cog in a well-oiled machine.

———

To become a truly proactive worker, we need to develop both a proactive workstyle and to protect ourselves against a potentially reactive environment. If we can improve our ability to work proactively while at the same time reduce the negative impact of our environment, our proactivity will be sure to increase.

So what next? Now that we have done some simple diagnosis and you have a sense of your workstyle and environment, how do we use this to reduce reactivity? Well, in the following chapters we are going to explore how to moderate urgency at both the personal and team levels. So, whether you are a worker, a manager or a leader, you will develop tools that contribute to creating a more proactive and productive culture.

URGENCY PLAYBOOK
<u>PRINCIPLE 2</u>

USE URGENCY WITH CARE

Urgency is a necessary tool to get traction and create momentum. But unnecessary urgency can be distracting for your team. Use urgency in a mindful, thoughtful and responsible way.

No matter what our position or role, we all wield a fair amount of power when it comes to urgency. Our actions can throw someone else's day into chaos. Our lack of planning can easily become a colleague's urgent problem. Our thoughtless last-minute request can pile unnecessary pressure and stress on a team member.

We often create unnecessary urgency without realising it. Because we are busy and probably a bit stretched ourselves, we create urgency and pass it on to others without thinking. To minimise this, we need to work on our awareness. We need to become more mindful of our behaviours and how they affect others. We need to try to work in a way that is productive for us personally, but also productive for those around us.

When urgency is necessary and unavoidable, then we need to be purposeful in the way we use it. This requires us to consider a few different things:

- If you are creating urgency for someone else, what is the best way to communicate it? Is an email enough, or should we have the courtesy to have a conversation with them? (Usually the latter.)

- What have they already got on their plate, and how can we understand this better and help them to reprioritise if necessary?

- What is the opportunity cost of what I am asking of them?

- Is my urgent request indicative of a pattern of behaviours or is it an exception?

You don't necessarily need to sit and ponder for an hour every time you have to ask somebody for something. I simply want to raise a new level of awareness for you that will subtly shift your behaviour. The more aware you are about how you work and the impact your behaviours have on others, the more likely you are to work in a way that avoids these situations if possible.

I personally hate pushing urgency on others, especially if it was avoidable. I am very aware of the occasions when I do it, and the rest of the time I use many proactive strategies to minimise unnecessary urgency. This is my mindset, and a part of my brand. People know this is the way that I work, and I hope that those who work closely with me are inspired to work in a similar way.

PART II
Minimise Personal Reactivity

Many of us make two mistakes when thinking about urgency. The first mistake is to believe your problem is *all* environmental; that you are operating in a reactive environment and that it is not at all about your own personal workstyle, habits and work preferences.

The second mistake is to believe that we cannot fix the problem of urgency. Julie Rynski, a senior executive with National Australia Bank, has likened this to the concept of 'learned helplessness'. People become victims of their environment and culture and feel they have no power to change things. This is incorrect, and in part II we will explore a range of strategies to combat this.

If you completed the urgency questionnaire (see figure 2.2 on pages 33–36) and scored poorly on the personal workstyle rating, you should pay special attention to this section. Urgency is a very personal issue. Even if you cannot change your environment, you can change how you work and behave. And habits can be changed, no matter how ingrained they are.

You, as an individual, are a product of your family, your upbringing, your environment, your experience and your beliefs. But your behaviours are a product of your habits. How you work is very much dictated by the tracks that have been carved over time in the floorboards of your working life. There are grooves that you travel along every day without even thinking about them, or how they affect the way you work, or indeed the results that you achieve.

Over time, it is very possible that you have developed a reactive workstyle without even being aware of it. You come in to work every day and deal with the deluge and the issues and the firefighting, and it feels normal. Not necessarily comfortable, but normal. The ruts you move back and forth in are well worn and are one less thing you have to think about.

But they are worth thinking about. Why?

Because comfortable does not equal productive.

Comfortable can create stress, for you and your colleagues. Comfortable can waste time. Think about how you tend to work. Think about your results in the urgency questionnaire. Is the reactivity you face all environmental or is there some room for improvement with your workstyle?

The good news is these comfortable grooves can be reshaped into more productive pathways. Your habits and behaviours can be shifted with a bit of focus and effort. And the results can be eye-opening!

Creating a proactive workstyle

A proactive workstyle can take effort to develop. As one of my clients pointed out, we tend to operate with what she called 'assignment syndrome', a behaviour learnt in school and at university. We learnt to leave assignments until the last minute, having convinced ourselves that we did our best work under pressure.

Now, we all know this was just a story we told ourselves to permit procrastination and a bit more partying. It did not lead to better results for most, and for many of us there came a time when we knew we had to buckle down or risk flunking out.

Creating a proactive workstyle requires two key ingredients (as shown in figure B):

1. **A proactive mindset.** Once developed, a proactive mindset becomes our default way of thinking, which means we are more likely to adopt proactive behaviours, especially when we get busy—which is when we need them the most.

2. **A proactive system.** The tools we use, and the systems we have set up to manage our work, are critical to proactively managing, planning and organising our work.

The combination of a proactive mindset and a proactive system leads to a proactive workstyle.

A workstyle that improves:

- how we work

- how we deal with others

- how our brand gets perceived in our organisation.

Imagine that: developing a brand where others know and trust not only the results that you deliver, but also the way you work. Sound good?

I think so too. Let's look at the strategies we can implement to do just that.

PROACTIVE MINDSET

How you think about your work

PROACTIVE SYSTEM

How you manage your work

PROACTIVE WORKSTYLE

Figure B: a proactive workstyle

CHAPTER 3

Develop a proactive mindset

I am inherently a proactive person, and believe I have a proactive mindset. Other people would say that about me. It's in my DNA, and it's just the way I think. I plan ahead. I try to anticipate future events and possibilities. I prepare now for later. I think about what other people will need from me and make sure I leave things in an appropriate state for them.

I also dislike reactivity immensely. I get frustrated when people leave things until the last minute and then cause me stress. I have crafted a business and a life that has very little urgency and reactivity in it. Of course, there will always be some urgency, but I minimise it as much as possible.

But it wasn't always this way.

As a teenager, and as a young adult, I was incredibly reactive. I never planned. I left things until the last minute. I rarely thought about leaving things in a reasonable state for others. And it was never my fault — it was always bad luck or someone else's fault when things went wrong.

Over the years, however, I have learnt to be more proactive and have felt the benefit of this way of thinking. I have developed a set of proactive principles that I operate by that are driven by my proactive mindset. These principles drive my behaviours. They are principles I have adopted and behaviours I've learnt. Combined, they inform the mindsets that I work with in relation to urgency.

I believe that being proactive is an investment in the future — my future. As they say, a stitch in time saves nine.

So regardless of how reactively you may be operating now — there is hope! It is fixable. You just need to know the right strategies to help you develop a more proactive mindset.

Mindset #1 — 'I plan ahead'

As much as I find this old saying a bit twee, it is true: 'failing to plan is planning to fail'. To work proactively, your first focus should be on planning. We know we should make time to plan, but most of us don't spend enough time doing this. Or at least doing it at the right level.

Many of us are a part of teams that plan at the organisational level, or the team level, or the project level. But few of us effectively link these big-picture plans with our day-to-day schedules. The irony is that we don't make time for this personal planning because we are too busy to stop! This is such a false economy. In *Smart Work*, I talk about *Organisational*-driven versus *You*-driven planning. You-driven planning is a personal routine at the monthly, weekly and daily level that drives important work into your schedule. This is one of the keys to dialling down urgency and spending more time on the proactive, important priorities that have impact.

I recommend developing the following personal planning routine:

- **daily planning** — 10 minutes each workday morning to get focused for the day

- **weekly planning** — 45 minutes once per week to get organised for the coming week(s)

- **monthly planning** — 1 hour at the start of each month to step back and get some perspective.

A key element of planning ahead is anticipation. Anticipation requires us to think about what will be needed down the track, or possible events that could arise that will be easier to handle with some forward planning.

Recently, for example, I experienced a highly urgent and possibly calamitous situation that was made much easier because of my proactive approach. I was flying from Sydney to the United States to work with one of my American clients. This was a big trip, with an important piece of work starting with the client. The flight to Dallas was long — 15 hours, and then a connecting flight to Arkansas.

As is my way, I packed the day before, and had a relaxed morning tying up a few loose ends before I left. I arrived at the airport about three hours before the flight, as suggested by the airline. Now, many businesspeople do not pay any attention to this and opt to sail as close to the wind as they can. They have meetings right up to the last minute and arrive in the nick of time to get through customs and board the plane. (Is that you?) Personally, I could never work that way. In fact, rather than work until the last minute before heading to the airport, I would prefer to arrive early and then do some work in the lounge.

Most of the time when I travel, the extra time I plan into my airport process is not necessary; it just gives me peace of mind, and allows me to be relaxed as I fly. But in this case, it actually saved my bacon.

I confidently handed my passport to the woman on the check-in desk. When she found my flight, she asked if I had a US visa. 'I sure do,' I replied, as I had been to the United States earlier in the year and had checked that my visa was valid for another 12 months. Her next question filled me with dread: 'For your *new* passport, sir? I can't find it in the system.'

I think my feet started to panic before my brain did. A cold feeling crept up my legs as I realised that I had ordered a new passport since my last US trip, and the visa I had was linked to my old passport. I had never even considered that I would have to update the visa application for this. It seems so obvious now, but it just never occurred to me.

'Is there anything I can do?' I asked.

'Yes,' she replied. 'Go over to the Flight Centre office by check-in counter G, and they should be able to apply online for you. It can take up to 72 hours, but I've seen them come through in an hour or two. You may be okay, but I can't guarantee it.'

So, with my heart in my mouth, I headed over to the Flight Centre office. I explained my predicament to a lovely young man called Dan. Turns out I was the seventh case he'd seen that morning. (It just shows how reactive we've all become!) He explained how many people get caught out in a situation like mine, or when transiting through the United States and not realising they need a visa. However, what he said next was the critical lesson.

'Lucky you came to the airport early. That gives us time to get this sorted.' I realised at that moment that if I had arrived an hour before the flight, I would have been up the creek without a paddle.

Thirty minutes and a coffee later, my approval came through and away I went. It was a moment of passing stress that could have been so much worse. So, I was glad that I arrived at the airport with plenty of time to spare. Now, if I were flying from Sydney to Melbourne, would I still arrive three hours beforehand? Maybe not, but then the risks would not be so great. If I missed a commuter flight to Melbourne, there would be another in 30 minutes or so. If I missed the flight to the United States, I would have to wait until the next day, and probably incur a greater expense. And the next day would have blown my schedule with the client.

The greater the risk, the more you should endeavour to be proactive.

Mindset #2—'I am responsive, not reactive'

We discuss this strategy in more detail in chapter 7, but it is worth a quick mention here within the context of mindset. Being responsive is very different from being reactive. People with reactive mindsets tend to be chaotic and stressful to work with. People with responsive mindsets are measured and organised, and usually a pleasure to work with. They don't just react to everything; they deal with things in a timely way. They prioritise and don't treat everything the same. When it is truly urgent they will be right on top of it, but when it's not as time sensitive they will deal with it in a timely way without dropping other important priorities.

They are also not afraid to negotiate and push back when necessary. And of course, to question why. For example, the other day I had lunch with one of my old clients who has stepped up into a senior role. It is a busy role in an organisation going through a lot of change. But she is not afraid to question why things are urgent: are they *really* urgent, and if so why? I love her mindset, and love working with her.

At times we are our own worst enemy, creating unnecessary urgency for ourselves. For instance, when work is delegated to us, or information is requested of us, we sometimes play the person, not the issue. By that I mean we assign urgency according to whom the request has come from, especially if it's from someone very senior, or from a key client.

One of the strategies for turning reactivity into responsiveness is to clarify expectations, and always ask when the work is needed.

If this is your mindset, it will be second nature to ask this. Every time. And after a while, it will become second nature for others to tell you without asking as they get used to your style. Joanne 'The Reactor' in chapter 1 could take a lesson from this one.

Mindset #3 — 'I pay it forward'

In the movie *Pay it Forward*, a young boy takes an unusual approach to a school assignment. When tasked with thinking of something that will change the world and putting it into action, he decides to pay favours forward rather than paying favours back. Rather than reacting to an act of kindness, he gets on the front foot to commit acts of kindness to others with no expectation of a returned favour. What a proactive act! If you believe in karma, you would know that this mindset pays itself back in the end.

Paying it forward is a key mindset when you are developing a proactive workstyle. It involves a more mindful approach that encourages you to think beyond your own needs, to the current and future needs of your colleagues. It involves thinking about how what you are doing may affect others, and making sure you are working in a way that makes life easier for them.

A simple but good example of this is my approach to toilet paper. Sorry to bring the conversation down, but this is such a good way of explaining the concept, so bear with me. When the toilet paper in the holder on the wall is finished, I replace it with a roll from the basket next to the toilet. When the basket next to the toilet has only one roll left, I replenish it from the packet in the cupboard. And when we're down to maybe six rolls in the cupboard, I buy some more. This means three things:

1. I never run out of toilet paper in the toilet or the house.

2. There is always a backup roll close at hand when the current roll does run out.

3. The next person to use the loo is never caught short. (You're welcome.)

This is automatic for me. I always make the effort to replenish now to save myself and others a problem in the future. This is the mark of a proactive mind.[21] How can you relate this to your work?

---

[21] This is a lesson I am still working on with my son.

How could you 'pay it forward' more in your role?

I really want this idea to make it out of the bathroom and into the wider workplace! I wonder if Julie—'The Last-Minute Delegator' from chapter 1—pays it forward when she is working with others?

Mindset #4—'I do it right the first time'

How much time is wasted in our workplaces when things are rushed and mistakes are made, leading to unnecessary rework? We are far too distracted these days, and often trying to do a hundred things at once. It's time for us to slow down again and develop a mindset where we do it right the first time.

An old builder's adage is 'measure twice, cut once'. It feels like we don't have time to slow down, but in the long run we save time if we do this. I would prefer to get fewer things done in a day, but to do the few critical things well and get them right. This is what we call effective. The person who gets lots of things done but makes lots of mistakes may feel efficient, but is not being effective. And the killer is, it's often others who bear the cost of this sloppiness.

When I bought my last laptop, I actually went to the brand's flagship store to pick it up. The tech assistant brought my shiny new device out, and offered to update Windows to the most current version for me. It seemed like a good idea to me, so I sat back while he did his work. As the new software downloaded, he flitted between me and a couple of other jobs, occasionally checking progress. After about 20 minutes the job was done, and off I went with my new computer. All good!

Except, when I got back to my office, I found the keyboard on the laptop no longer worked. Nothing I did could get it working! *Grrr...*

So, the following day I was back in store, reporting my problem. The tech guy I got on this day knew exactly what the problem was; he told me with a smile that new drivers needed to be installed. He suggested that the other guy should have done this, as this was a known problem when updating Windows. *Double Grrr...*

Now, at one level being angry about this sounds petty. The guy made a mistake — give him a break. He was busy and missed a step. Maybe. But at another level, a more productive level, he should have made sure he did it right first time, saving me time and angst, and of course the time and effort of his colleague to fix the error. So, what could he have done differently to avoid the mistake?

Firstly, he could have focused on one job, rather than splitting his concentration across three. Secondly, he could have just slowed down a bit, and as he completed the job, done a quick mental check that he had covered all the steps, and a quick physical check that all was working. If it was a complex job, or he was unfamiliar with it, he could have used a checklist. All simple things that make sure we get it right the first time.

This is a sad example of what happens in our busy workplaces *every day*. We rush work because we're under pressure and end up costing ourselves and others precious time.

We need to work in a mindful way, which means we need to slow down to speed up.

Mindset #5 — 'I prioritise by importance, not urgency'

We like to see ourselves as evolved workers, but the truth is many of us approach work like a Neanderthal. To illustrate, today I had a 'discretionary' morning: no meetings until 3 pm. It's a Friday during school holidays, so I thought it would be relatively quiet and interruption free: a blank canvas to get stuff done.

I had lots of things to do, but three things immediately stood out:

1. I needed to draft a project outline for a client that was due today. (My *'must do'* priority.)

2. I would like to upgrade to the new iPhone. (My *'like to do'* priority.)

3. I had to complete a major proposal for a training rollout with a new client. (This is not urgent, but very high value — my *'should do'* priority.)

Now, my caveman brain was torn. It wanted to follow its primal desires. So, my first instinct was to order the new iPhone first.

But wait, stop! Somewhere down in the depths of my evolved brain, I heard, 'Do the right thing, Dermot'. It was telling me to do what I *should* do first, not what I felt like doing first. So I reprioritised and played a game with myself. Here was the running order in the end.

Firstly, I did the thing I *should* do first: I wrote and sent the proposal. I did the most important thing first. I then rewarded myself by doing the thing I really wanted to do — I ordered the iPhone. A nice little reward that reinforced this behaviour for next time. I then did the urgent priority, which might have been time sensitive, but was not so urgent that it could not wait a couple of hours. Whew! After all that activity I needed a nap!

Back in our cave-dwelling past, humans did not have that many things to remember, think about or to do compared to today. Their basic prioritisation system was appropriate and ensured the survival of the fittest. But today we have too much information, and many competing priorities. We need a more evolved way of thinking to survive in this environment.

Much of our time can be caught up dealing with the urgent stuff, or the easy stuff, or the fun stuff. But a proactive mindset focuses on the important stuff first. I believe that people who consistently prioritise the important over the urgent not only survive, but actually thrive.

I ask you to consider, with the greatest respect, whether you are a bit of a Neanderthal sometimes.

Mindset #6 — 'I minimise procrastination'

There is an old saying that goes something like 'Why put off to tomorrow what you can do today?' This is a great ideal designed to reduce procrastination. If you can do it today, you should. But maybe this saying was crafted in a different era, when lords and ladies had time on their hands, and needed to fill the lazy days in between parties and duels. I am being a bit facetious here, but the working world has changed, and I reckon many of us act with another option in mind — 'Why do today what you can put off until tomorrow? If it can wait, it should.'

I reckon both options are valid in today's busy world. The key is putting off the right things until later, and making sure you don't procrastinate the important things.

To be honest, one of my productivity weaknesses is procrastination. I have so many ideas and great intentions, but sometimes I just don't feel like doing some things. I'll procrastinate when things are hard or complicated. If I have a complicated invoice to itemize, which includes travel receipts and multiple destinations, watch out. I could sit on that one for months!

I find it very easy to procrastinate when there is no external pressure. By that I mean things that I want to drive forward, but no-one else is asking for. Writing this book is a great example of this. This is my idea, and my passionate 'soapbox' subject. No-one, and I mean *no-one*, has asked me to write a book on urgency. But it is an issue that I see every day, and I know that this could help, so I decided I should write it.

But there is a big difference between deciding that I should write it and actually putting fingers to keys and hammering it out. In fact, my first book, *Smart Work*, took me over 10 years from writing the opening paragraph to publishing it. I started by wanting to be an author, but without any external pressure to write, I lost focus and procrastinated. For over 10 years!

So when I decided to write *Urgent!* I started to gather ideas. I bought a nice red[22] notebook, and jotted down lots of notes and thoughts. As I mentioned in the introduction, I even started writing in a moment of inspiration on the Cinque Terre. But then I felt the familiar tap of Mr Procrastination on my shoulder. 'You're busy', he said. 'You don't have time to write a book this year. Wait until next year.'

---

[22] Red to remind me of urgency!

I knew I needed to silence Mr Procrastination. So, I set myself a deadline. Actually, even better, I got someone else to set a deadline for me that I could not ignore. I emailed my publishing editor, Lucy, and pitched the book to her. I knew that if Lucy liked the idea, and her editing team agreed that this book had legs, she would give me a deadline. Sure enough, a couple of weeks later I got the thumbs up, and a hard deadline. And now I am carried relentlessly along on a roller-coaster that I cannot control. All I can do is write, and know that the roller-coaster arrives back in the station on the deadline date.

This is a great way of mobilising myself to get traction with a piece of work that, if left undone, would not be picked up by anyone else.

I reckon that we often put off the things that we know are important, but have no external pressure applied to them. We prioritise what we class as 'urgent' over our proactive work on a regular basis. But highly effective people learn to drive their priorities forward by creating a sense of urgency for themselves and others when something is important. Setting deadlines is a part of this. But personal deadlines can be easily broken; deadlines that are public hold us more accountable. I knew an email to Lucy would force my hand and require me to follow through. Be aware of your comfortable behaviours, and have strategies in place to force yourself into more productive behaviours.

Jing — 'The Procrastinator' in chapter 1 — was very comfortable with her behaviours, but did not perform as well as she could have.

Know thyself, and then implement plans to force yourself to act on the things that have impact.

Mindset #7 — 'I think several steps ahead'

As some of you may know from my previous books, I am a bit of a soccer hack. I play over-45 soccer[23] for my local club with a bunch of old blokes. We are in the lowest division of the oldest age group in the area, and we love it. We might not be able to score many goals, but we can still open a beer afterwards without too much trouble, and we'll keep going until we can't!

I coached soccer for a time when my son was young, so I know a few things about the game even if I can't execute them well myself. One of the things I learned over the years was how to pass and receive the ball. When you get to my age, the key to passing is to pass the ball to the other player's feet, as they usually can't move more than a metre or so either side if you're inaccurate. Inflexible muscles and slow minds!

While accurate passing is important, I think how you receive the ball is even more critical. When you see a great player receive a pass, it looks effortless, as if the ball is a part of their body. But it takes practice, and a proactive approach to playing the game.

I reckon there are five levels of receiving the ball, moving from bad to great, and they're all relevant to how we work:

Level 1: Look the other way

This is where the player that the ball is being passed to isn't even looking in the right direction, and the ball ends up bouncing off the back of their legs, probably into your own goal or to one

---

[23] Okay, 'football' if you must! In Ireland football was called soccer to avoid confusion between Gaelic football and English football.

of the opposition players. Not a good look, but common at the under-six level, as well as the over-45 level!

Are you sometimes figuratively looking the other way with your work? Are you sometimes so caught up with your own busy-ness that you completely miss things?

Level 2: Kick blindly

Level 2 involves the receiving player seeing the pass, but then just booting it blindly once they get it. They probably panic, and have no awareness of who is around them, what options they have or what pressure they are under. They just have a knee-jerk reaction and get the ball away as quickly as they can.

Do you sometimes just react to a request without thinking about the options available or the best approach to the work?

Level 3: Receive and then look up

You will often hear soccer coaches shout 'Head up!' This is designed to get the player to lift their eyes off the ball for a moment to take a look at what's happening around them, and what options they might have. This is good, but still not ideal because by the time you have received the ball and then looked up, you already have an opposition player on top of you. Too late.

Are you sometimes so overwhelmed by work that even when your colleagues try to help, it's too hard or too late?

Level 4: Look up before receiving

This is much better. Good players have it drilled into them to look around quickly as the ball is being passed to them. This allows them to see their options early, make a decision and know what they're going to do once they receive the ball. This is a great example of a proactive strategy that improves the quality of your decision making and work.

Do you have the mental space to start thinking a few steps ahead to make your work more proactive and less reactive?

Level 5: Anticipate future possibilities

The really great players, the ones who not only have innate talent but have also practised and trained for long periods with a team, go to level 5. This is where they look up before receiving the ball, so they can read what is happening, but they also anticipate what is likely to happen several steps ahead because they have practised drills and set-plays over and over with their teammates.

Are you aligned and in tune with your team so you can anticipate what they are likely to do in reactive situations? Are they in tune with you?

————

As we go up the levels, we see a more proactive approach being taken. More time is invested in assessing the environment and situation, allowing for better decision making and execution. This is easy to do when there is no pressure, but hard to do when we're under pressure.

You don't need to play soccer to see how this analogy works. It's probably true of most team sports, and it's certainly true in all workplaces. This mindset may be uncomfortable for you at first, as we are used to just going at a million miles an hour, but with mindful practice it can really shift your behaviours.

At a personal level, your mindset is so important in shaping how you work. It is your choice.

Do you want to work with a reactive mindset, or a proactive one?

But as we have seen, mindset is only half of the equation when it comes to developing a proactive workstyle. The other half of the equation is the system we use to manage our work.

URGENCY PLAYBOOK
<u>PRINCIPLE 3</u>

AVOID CREATING UNNECESSARY URGENCY FOR OTHERS

Don't leave work until it's urgent, and then push urgency onto others if you need their input. Lack of planning on your part should not cause a crisis for them.

As we have already discussed, so much urgency in the workplace is avoidable. We:

- leave things until the last minute

- forget things until someone chases us

- get overwhelmed by our inboxes and let things slip

- make things more urgent than they need to be.

If we want to avoid creating unnecessary urgency, we need to work proactively. This requires a proactive planning system to manage our time, commitments and priorities. It requires that we have a balanced approach to our work, and not spend most of our day in meetings with no time left to get priorities done. It requires us to stay on top of things like our inbox. It requires us to have some flexibility in our schedule and to be aware of our changing priorities.

Working proactively takes effort. It requires a good planning system and good planning processes that are regularly practised. But it is worth it: you will benefit personally, and the people around you will benefit too. Nobody likes to work with a chaotic, disorganised and reactive manager. They will put up with it for a while, but eventually they'll move on to somewhere that allows them some control over their time.

Your workstyle, especially if you are a manager or a leader, sets the tone for the culture of your team. You get to choose whether it is a positive one or a negative one.

CHAPTER 4
Working proactively

Once we have developed a proactive mindset, we need proactive strategies and systems in place to support it. Why? Well, it's one thing to have good intentions, and another to act on them. Good systems help with that. If we reduce the friction that can get in the way of working proactively, there is less risk of slipping back into reactive behaviours. And a workload management system that promotes reactivity over proactivity will create friction for you.

My friend Cameron Schwab, who has many years' experience in Australian rules football administration, talks about the idea that in footy, it's not necessarily the best team that will win; it's the best system. Footy is a reactive game, with lots of unknowns, like the unpredictable bounce of the ball or the impact of a tackle. But good systems help players to manage the unpredictability.

When it comes to how we organise ourselves, we can use systems that help us to work proactively or force us to work reactively. I see a lot of people using inadequate productivity systems that lead them to work reactively in one of two ways — what I call first-minute reactivity and last-minute reactivity.[24]

First–minute reactivity

When we do things at the first minute, we are usually reacting to things such as email alerts, ringing phones or physical interruptions. These things are often not actually urgent, but we react anyway because they are immediate and persistent. Think about a ringing phone — it's hard to ignore. Emails are an especially intrusive and distracting form of incoming work, and I believe they are responsible in part for the dramatic rise of urgency in the workplace.

Over the last two decades, as email has become more and more prevalent, we have developed poor habits around it that cause us to work more reactively than we should for no good reason. We tell ourselves we are keeping things moving, and that we are working efficiently by responding quickly, but the reality is that while we might be efficient, we are not being effective.

Add to this the distraction and pull of our always present mobile devices, and you have a perfect storm of interruption and distraction. This all drives a sense of urgency that is not real. But it is destructive. And it is self-inflicted.

Last-minute reactivity

We can also spend too much time working on things at the last minute if we are not careful. For instance, we might receive emails that we look at but leave in our inbox to deal with later.

[24] I also refer to this in chapter 2, where we examine our urgency workstyle.

But once that email gets buried by newer ones, there is a risk that it will slip through the cracks. That is, until someone has to chase us for the response a week later when it has become urgent. We then need to drop what we were doing to deal with the urgent item, derailing our priorities for the day and possibly putting unnecessary pressure on others.

This is a very common workstyle; in fact, as mentioned previously, some people revel in this way of working. They say that they don't bother to do things until they are urgent enough. They don't mind the increased pressure or stress, and in some ways enjoy it. But the reality is that working this way just increases mistakes, rework and stress for you and those around you.

The solution to both of these reactive behaviours is to work as much as possible in the proactive zone, as figure 4.1 (overleaf) shows. Our productivity is higher when we work in this zone rather than in the first-minute or last-minute zones.

The proactive zone

In the story of Goldilocks and the Three Bears, Goldilocks preferred the middle chair, bed and bowl of porridge. Not too hot, not too cold — just right. Working in the proactive zone is similar. Not too soon, not too late — just right.

I find that people work more proactively if they schedule their work using a time-based system. This forces you to choose a day or time to work on a priority that is not right now, but also not at the last minute.

It also requires that you have a system that makes all of your other commitments and priorities visible so you can tell if you are over-committing yourself.

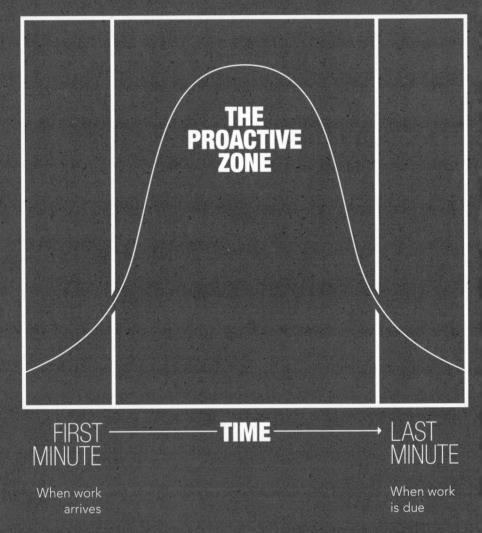

THE
PROACTIVE
ZONE

FIRST ——— **TIME**———➤ LAST
MINUTE   MINUTE

When work   When work
arrives   is due

Figure 4.1: the proactive zone

The challenge is that in my experience most people don't have personal productivity systems set up to do this. We might schedule our meetings and block some time out in the calendar for bigger chunks of work. But most priorities are just listed in our to-do list, left in our overflowing inbox, or managed in our head. This reactive system just does not cut the mustard.

Working with a proactive schedule

I worry that your productivity system is outdated. Think about the tools you use to manage your commitments and priorities. Chances are, if you're like most people in the corporate workplace, you're using an electronic calendar to manage your meetings. This is a reasonably proactive tool because it is time based, and allows you to schedule your commitments ahead of time.

But now think about your tools for managing priorities and tasks. If you're like many people you may still use a paper to-do list.

A to-do list is a good way of making things visible and ensuring that they do not get forgotten. But remember a list is just a pile of work, with no time associated with the activities.

A to-do list can lead to the most pressing tasks being done first, with less urgent actions being left until later. There is rarely any time attached to the actions in the list, which means that many of us just scan the list for the most urgent items and attack those first. Our work therefore gets prioritised by urgency, rather than by importance.

I believe we need more proactive action systems in place if we want to work more proactively. The following are five recommendations that will transform your current system into a far more proactive platform for managing your work.

1. Use one central system for actions

If you think about all of the actions and priorities you currently have on your plate, chances are these items sit in many different places. Some of the things you need to do are in your inbox, some in your to-do list, some in your meeting notebook, possibly some in a project Excel spreadsheet, and probably many are just in your head. We tend to fragment our work and put it in different piles, depending on how it arrived to us, or how the action was captured.

The problem with this way of working is twofold:

1. It is very hard to prioritise your work effectively if it is buried in lots of different places.

2. It is also very hard to manage your work proactively around this stuff because none of the tools I mentioned are designed to manage your time.

My advice to you is to create one place where you manage all of your priorities and commitments. Most of the modern email and calendar tools used in organisations like yours, such as MS Outlook and Gmail, have the ability to bring your tasks into the same view as your meetings. You can usually set up a split view that would show your tasks either on the side of your calendar view, or above or below your meetings for the week. The combining of your meetings and tasks into one view gives you more visibility and control over your work.

If you put all of your eggs into the one basket, and commit to using your electronic calendar for all of your meetings, and your electronic task list for all of your priorities, you will create a more holistic and useful view of your workload. One that promotes working more proactively.[25]

2. Manage activities by time

Next, start to manage your priorities by time. This requires scheduling the things you need to do in a proactive way. Don't do everything the minute it comes in, and don't leave things until the last minute. Decide when you are going to do things and schedule time for them in the proactive zone.

This may mean that you block time out in your calendar for this activity, which is a good strategy for bigger chunks of work, as you are protecting that time as well as scheduling it. But it could also mean that you just schedule a task for the appropriate day in your schedule. This is a more flexible approach to task workload, as it allows you to schedule the work in your list for that day, without having to lock it into a particular time.

For instance, I may have a proposal that I need to concentrate on for a couple of hours blocked out in my calendar. But I may also have a follow-up phone call to a client scheduled as a task to be done at some stage today, but not necessarily at a specific time.

Tools such as MS Outlook, Google Calendar and Lotus Notes all allow you to date-activate tasks to appear on the relevant

---

[25] I discuss this concept more fully in my first book, *Smart Work*.

day in your system, allowing you to create lists of things to be done today or tomorrow, this week or next week.

This is a simple but effective system for managing priorities. It forces you to think more proactively about when you will do things, and it allows you to manage your time more holistically, as you can get a better feel of your capacity when you look at your meetings and priorities together. They both need time to get done, so doesn't it make sense to manage them together?

> **Scheduling your work proactively is one of the easiest but most powerful ways to shift your mindset away from urgency and towards importance.**

Another consideration when scheduling task workload is whether you focus on the due date of the task, or the start date. Most electronic task systems have the tasks sorted by due date. But I reckon this just feeds into the last-minute mindset. I prefer to change the sorting to the start date, so that I'm always thinking about when I'm going to *start* work, not just finish it.

3. Highlight three critical priorities each day

One of the benefits of planning your work in this way is focus. When your work is visible in one system, it can help you to really focus on what needs to get done. One of the tricks that I recommend that will help you to focus even more on what is most important is to highlight three critical priorities each day, and fight for them. These actions could be time-sensitive things that must get done, or important proactive things that would be worth doing. Either way, you should elevate them by highlighting them as critical.

It amazes me how much urgency has come to represent what we call a priority. But as Stephen Covey suggested in *First Things First*, a priority has both an urgent and an important component. Just like both aerobic and anaerobic[26] fitness is needed to perform at high levels in many sports, so importance and urgency are often needed to move work forward productively. Importance is like aerobic fitness, as it has a more long-term focus; urgency is like the chemical reaction in anaerobic fitness. Both are critical to success in the workplace.

In fact, when I am thinking about priorities, I like to think in terms of criticality. It looks something like this:

Importance × Urgency = Criticality

The criticality of a task is a combination of the amount of impact the activity will have on my goals and objectives, or for the team or business around me, combined with the time-sensitivity of the task. If I consider both aspects of the work, I will be making a more informed judgement on how and when I do the work.

So on a daily basis I highlight three critical priorities in my task list. These are my main focus for the day alongside my meetings. On a weekly basis I consider my critical activities for the week ahead. And on a monthly basis I identify ten big, critical priorities for the month ahead.[27] Each time I'm considering both urgency and importance, and I'm giving the critical activities some form of prominence in my planning system.

---

[26] Aerobic fitness is how the body uses oxygen in the blood to create energy and is good for stamina and endurance. Anaerobic fitness helps the body to convert chemicals in the muscles for short, sharp bursts of energy, which is good for sprinting, amongst other things.

[27] See 'Mindset #1 — I plan' ahead on page 54.

4. Balance your time

Having suggested that you set up a proactive action management system, let me talk about one of the biggest mistakes I see when busy people start using a system like this: they don't balance their time effectively.

I have suggested that your week is made up of time spent on a series of meetings and priorities, and that they all need time to be completed. But there is no point in scheduling your tasks into a proactive system if you do not *protect* the time to do them!

I work with many senior managers who love the idea of using this system to get in control of the busy workloads, but fail miserably because they give 90 per cent of their time away to meetings, and never have any time left over to get the priorities done — at least not during working hours. They often leave the tasks for after 6 pm and throw their work–life balance out of whack.

My advice for you if you have a busy meeting schedule is to set a cap on your meeting time. Decide how much time you are willing to devote to meetings each week, and cap it at that. Protect the rest of your time for priorities and administration such as email management.

One manager I worked with estimated she was spending 80 per cent of her week in meetings, which was unacceptable. She worked on setting a cap of 60 per cent of her time for meetings, and became more discerning about the meetings she accepted. Suddenly she had a lot more time to get stuff done during core working hours. Who knew?

5. Turn off email alerts

This is book number three for me, yet in each book I have felt the need to make this point. I also know I've already brought it up in this book. And I feel frustrated that I need to keep making this point. But I do, because I still see so many people who have email alerts going off on their laptop and on their phone when an email arrives.

You really don't need to know every time an email comes in. In fact, your productivity takes a hit when you are distracted so much by often irrelevant communications. Go to the settings menu in your email tool and on your phone, and turn off the alerts. If you must, you could set up specific alerts for the key people you deal with, such as your manager, so that you get an alert if they email you.

Tell your wider group of colleagues that this is your strategy to remain focused, and agree on a communication method that can be used if cut-through is needed for something truly urgent. Ask them to talk to you directly, or maybe send a text. This is a system change, but also a mindset change. It links directly to chapter 3's 'Mindset #2 — I am responsive, not reactive'.

————

Obviously, the recommendations here are brief and high level. If you feel you need extra help in this area, I recommend doing some deeper reading on the subject of personal productivity. Make sure the book or course is up to date and relevant to the modern workplace. And take some time to change your behaviours.

I usually find it takes at least four weeks of concerted effort with a new system or skillset for it to become comfortable and for you to see the benefits.

So now that you have a proactive system in place let's have a look at how we can deal with all those urgent issues that are going to be thrown at you. Let's learn to negotiate.

URGENCY PLAYBOOK
<u>PRINCIPLE 4</u>

TELL THEM WHEN YOU NEED IT BY

Don't assume that others will know when you need work back by. Always clearly state the deadline when requesting work and open the space for negotiation if needed.

When we are busy and moving at a million miles an hour, it's too easy to half-delegate work. We:

- send an email asking for a report

- ask our assistant to book a meeting with a client

- tell them *what* we want, but sometimes we don't take the time to tell them *when* we need it by.

The challenge with this is not just that they may put it off and delay the work.

I find that too often, especially if you're a senior manager, they may assume urgency when it's not there at all. You might need a report before a meeting next week, and send a request to one of your analysts. The report lands on your desk that afternoon. Great, one less thing to worry about—what awesome service! But you need to ask yourself what other priority was dropped to rush your work through. Or you may need to question the quality of the product if it was done so quickly.

You are far better off building a habit around communicating clear and reasonable deadlines, and setting an expectation that everyone in the team do this. And if someone requests work without a clear deadline, set the expectation that the other party clarifies the deadline before commencing work. This is basic stuff that, if done consistently, has a huge impact on team productivity.

CHAPTER 5
Negotiating urgency

I was working recently on a project with Chauntelle, my business manager, to develop some new training resources. We had a meeting and discussed the outcome we would like to achieve, roughly what these resources would look like and how they would work.

After the meeting I decided it would be great to have the resources ready for a session that I would be running in the United States a few weeks later. I emailed Chauntelle and suggested this might be a good deadline to aim for. I could hear the gears turning in her mind as she thought about working to such a tight time frame, but she trusts me, so she replied, 'Let's go for it', And off we went. We decided to do the design in-house to save time, so Chauntelle got onto it right away.

A few days later she sent through her initial designs and, unfortunately, they were not quite what I was expecting. I immediately realised that by putting pressure on the deadline (reducing the time available), I had inadvertently reduced the quality of the design. She had to work on something that was beyond her experience level, on top of her already busy workload.

Upon realising my error, I called her and thanked her for the first draft but recommended that we let go of the US deadline, which was a 'nice to have' deadline rather than a 'drop dead' deadline. I also suggested that we now had time to bring an external designer into play. I could sense the relief that she felt—she thought that was a top idea. I realised that the most important outcome for me in the project was the quality. I wanted these resources to look and feel amazing, and was willing to wait, and even pay a bit more, to achieve that.

The lesson for me was that sometimes when you apply urgency pressure, it becomes a constraint that can affect other aspects of the work. This has become one of my key strategies for moderating urgency.

Project managers have long used a concept to help them plan, monitor and control their projects called the 'triple constraint'. In most scenarios these constraints (or variables) are time, cost and scope, with quality sometimes also thrown into the mix. The analogy often used to explain the concept is 'you can have it fast, cheap or good—choose two'. Each constraint, if changed, will affect the other constraints in some way.

A constraint is a limitation or restriction, which in this context is going to dictate how or when work is done.

Project managers can use these constraints as indicators of issues within the project, or as a way of controlling competing demands on the project. So in project terms, if the deadline for the project has been brought forward by management, then the project manager can attempt to meet the shorter deadline by reducing the quality of the output, or increasing the cost of the project by bringing in more external resources. Equally, if the scope of a project increases because management want to include an additional report in the deliverables, the project manager could accommodate this by negotiating an extended deadline or could draft additional resources to work on the report. The constraints are interdependent and can be very useful in managing complex and competing priorities.

The six dials

In recent years the PMBOK (Project Management Body of Knowledge) guide to project management has broadened this list to six constraints, upon which I have loosely based the idea the dials that managers can use to moderate urgency.

The six dials you can use to moderate urgency are:

1. time

2. quality

3. scope

4. resources

5. budget

6. risk.

One of the phrases I've found myself using a lot as I talk about the urgency issue is that you need to 'dial the urgency down a bit'.

I like the idea of turning dials up and down to control these variables to get the balance right, just like the knobs you might turn on a music amplifier to adjust the sound. These are not on/off switches, but controls with a range of different settings, from low to high (see figure 5.1, overleaf).

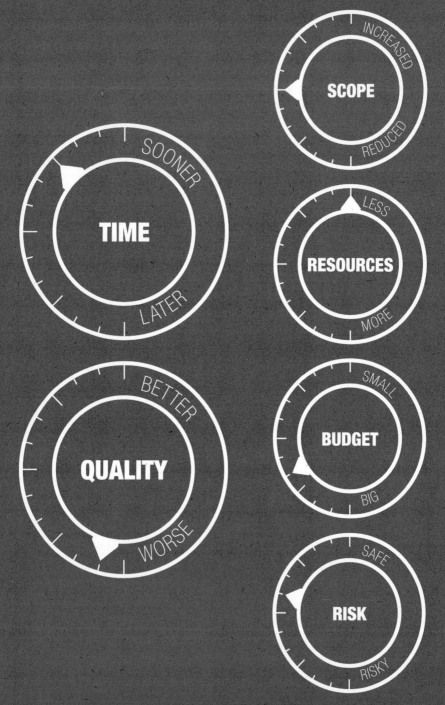

Figure 5.1: six urgency dials

When a constraint has been set by the business or a customer, these controls can be adjusted to help you to negotiate the best way of achieving the desired outcomes. For example, a leader observes that one of her team members has been under the pump for a couple of months with urgent deadlines, and is now operating in the reactive zone. Acute and chronic reactivity has set in. She might decide to review what the team member is working on and see if she could take some things off their plate, or reduce the scope of some of their projects to ease the pressure.

These are just some of the options available to the manager. This requires a high level of awareness from the manager, and a belief that things within their control could reduce the load on their team. If they can bring the team member back down into the active zone, they will avoid possible burnout down the track.

Let's look at each of the dials and see how they could be used to negotiate urgency with others.

Dial #1: time

Sooner—later

Time is obviously the main constraint we are focused on in this book. Or at least the lack (or perceived lack) of time, which leads to urgency. If time is at stake, all of the other constraints can be dialled up or down to increase or decrease the urgency involved.

Of course, you might decide to adjust the time dial itself to ease or increase pressure.

If I'm totally honest, I used this dial myself when writing this book. I had a final manuscript date that landed just after Christmas. At the time it was set this felt like a good date, as

I would be quiet with work over that time and had no holiday scheduled. But then we bought a new house and the move also landed over the Christmas period. Suddenly I was very distracted by the move and finding it hard to focus on the writing as I should have.

As my deadline loomed, I emailed Lucy, my publishing editor, to see if there was some wiggle room with the date. Luckily there was, and I got another few weeks, which was all I needed. I took the pressure off myself by asking the question and adjusting the time dial. But if time is not negotiable, it's the other dials that will need to be adjusted.

Dial #2: quality

Better—worse

Time and quality are often the most obvious dials used to control urgency, hence their prominence in figure 5.1. We all want to deliver a quality outcome when we work. But sometimes good enough is good enough—perfect does not serve. So, we need to be aware that we will put pressure on the deadline if we increase the quality required. But inversely, a way to decrease pressure would be to lessen the required quality. This would make it easier for the individual or team to deliver the output on the deadline alongside their other priorities. This does not mean that we should produce poor-quality work; just that we consider and negotiate what 'good enough' looks like and what would be acceptable.

One CEO I worked with in the United States who managed a very large retail business coached her team to work on the premise that 80 per cent was usually good enough. She did not want them wasting time on perfection when 80 per cent would be perfectly acceptable for the stakeholders involved.

This again can be a useful negotiating tool.

Ask the question of your stakeholders—what does good enough look like?

Don't make assumptions about what level of quality they need. You may find that it is actually lower than you think.

Dial #3: scope
Increased—reduced

Scope is about the deliverables required within a piece of work. Everything that needs to be produced and handed over by the deadline is considered to be 'in scope'. For example, you may be working on a major consulting proposal for a client, which might include:

- an executive summary

- the proposal itself

- a statement of work

- a sample methodology document

- a slide deck for the proposal presentation.

In this example, other priorities within the team may be putting pressure on the deadline (which cannot be moved as it involves the presentation to the client leadership team). So, the decision is made that the scope of the work could be reduced by leaving the creation of the sample methodology document until after the presentation, as it is not critical to the success of the proposal.

My partner, Vera, found this a useful solution during a particularly busy period in her role. Her team were preparing a quarterly finance report for their regional head office in Singapore. The report had almost 20 detailed components, which was very time consuming to prepare, especially on top of their usual finance work at the time. A conversation with her boss in Singapore highlighted that several of the components were not actually used in their review process anymore, so could probably be left out. This saved her team valuable time and allowed them to ensure that the report they sent was correct and accurate.

Another way to look at this concept is to reduce the scope of what one of your team members has on their plate to reduce pressure. By sitting down with them and going through the priorities they have on their list, you could either kill some non-critical priorities altogether, push out their deadlines or assign some of the tasks to others. This reduces their scope of work and allows them to focus on the critical deadline. It is crucial that you include this type of workload review in your regular one-on-ones. It might be time consuming for you, and tedious for them, but it helps to keep them focused and on top of what matters.

Dial #4: resources

Less—more

Cameron Schwab shared with me that the best quote he ever heard about strategy was along the lines of 'strategy is about making the best use of scarce resources'. Human, and to a lesser extent physical, resources are definitely tools that we can use to increase or decrease the pressure of urgency.

Very simply, if a team is under constant pressure, either bring in additional resources to assist, or reallocate other resources that are not working at capacity to help out. Conversely, by taking away resources you can increase urgency.

One of the advantages of using multiple resources on a job is the power of concurrency. Person 1 can be working on task A and person 2 can be working on task B simultaneously, therefore reducing the overall time needed.

I fear that sometimes we adopt a mindset where we must do all the work ourselves. We don't spot the opportunities to save time by delegating some of the work to others, or we're so busy that we don't make the time to delegate, ending up in a situation where we have to do it all ourselves.

The key with this is to be aware of the capacity of your team, and each individual in the team.

Agile is a project management methodology that has become very popular in recent years, known for its stand-up huddles that are run each morning around a bunch of sticky notes on a board. One of the key outcomes of this, when done well, is a much clearer understanding of blockages in the workflow, and the capacity of the team to get the work done.

These teams will often use a technique called 'swarming', where the whole teams swarms around a piece of work that is getting stuck or running behind. They work together to get it moving and then get back to their other tasks. These problem tasks are identified in their morning meetings, so the managers involved have a real sense of where everything is at, and what people are working on.

You don't need to use agile project management to take advantage of this concept to allocate your resources better.

Dial #5: budget
Small—big

Money is the solution to all problems—or at least that's what some people think. For me it's not the answer to all woes, but it does help. It gives you flexibility; things can be sped up (or slowed down for that matter) if enough money is thrown at them. A good example of this was a major presentation I ran at a client conference. We had been working on a set of new resources that I realised would be perfect as a handout for the session.

However, the design took longer than anticipated, and it looked like we were not going to have them ready for the conference. Unlike the US gig that I mentioned at the start of this chapter, I really wanted these resources for this session as I knew they would create great impact and could make or break the session. So we looked into delivery options, and it turned out that we could save time by delivering them directly to the conference from the printer in Hong Kong. They would need to be airfreighted, and that was not cheap, but I made the decision that the impact would be worth it.

So, by spending more money we were able to deliver on time. Now, this is not how I want to run my business, leaving things until the last minute and then just throwing money at the problem. It would not make a very profitable business model.

> **But when it is the exception, and the increased budget is used in a purposeful way, it is acceptable.**

In a corporate environment, increased spending usually equates to outsourcing work to external parties or services. This is an option that can be used in some situations, and it is always worth having an idea of the providers that could be used if this requirement arises.

Dial #6: risk
Low—high

Finally, there is the risk appetite that you, or your organisation, are willing to tolerate. When you want to reduce risk as much as possible, you may be creating a high level of urgency in order to meet the deadline. Or in some cases reducing risk means slowing down; it depends on the situation. If you are willing to tolerate a bit of risk, you can speed things up and even cut a few corners.

Your risk appetite can set the tone around urgency. One of my mentors will not be forced into making fast decisions around important issues. He says that if you want a quick decision, the answer is 'No'. That communicates to me that if you want his decision, you cannot come in at the last minute and expect a quick turnaround.

I do a lot of work in the banking and finance sector in Australia. If you're reading this in Australia you'll be very familiar with the Royal Commission into the banking industry in this country, and the resultant implications for the major banks. There have been huge fines levied on some of the banks for breaches in conduct with customers. The banks are now making reforms that will ensure these breaches will not happen again, and it has led to a huge reduction in risk appetite in some of these organisations. Leadership are mandating that all the i's are dotted and the t's crossed to minimise risk. This is a massive change in culture—for the better, I believe, and I think that learning to moderate urgency will be part of the solution for them.

A final thought on risk in relation to urgency. The higher the risk involved, the more proactively you should work. Leaving things until the last minute is fine if the risk is low. But when it is high, it makes sense to plan well and work as proactively as you can. If I have a workshop in another city that starts at 9 am, I will always fly the night before, just in case of bad weather or delays. It does not do to have 12 people sitting in a room waiting for the facilitator.[28] But if I have a client meeting starting at 9 am, I might be more open to risk flying down that morning, as the consequences are not so great if I am late.

————

These urgency dials are an innovative way to moderate urgency as an individual. They provide a simple framework to work out the best way to deal with any looming deadline or urgent issue. They give you agency and the ability to take control. They provide flexibility and the ability to manage many competing priorities and deadlines. And they give you a balanced way to dial urgency up or down without killing your team.

How could you use the six urgency controls with some of the current deadlines you and your team are struggling to meet?

---

[28] Especially when he is a productivity expert!

Understand the non-negotiables for your stakeholders

A final note about the six urgency controls. They can be a very useful negotiation tool when dealing with clients or other stakeholders in your organisation. In fact, I see them as a critical way to understand what is important to your stakeholders. Understand what their absolute non-negotiable constraint would be. Ask them the question, as it will help you to manage their expectations.

If you are delivering a work request, a project or a product, ask each key stakeholder what their most important constraint is. For some it may be the deadline. They don't care if it costs more, or needs to have a slightly smaller scope, or even slightly lower quality. But they want it delivered on time. Understanding why may also be useful for you and your team; it provides the context for them to make sure they deliver.

Another stakeholder may feel that the deadline could slip a bit, but they will not compromise on the cost. Obviously, you may find that everyone has a different need, and you cannot please everyone. But understanding these needs helps you to make better decisions and to negotiate with your stakeholders. That's got to be a good thing!

URGENCY PLAYBOOK
<u>PRINCIPLE 5</u>

DON'T ALWAYS EXPECT
INSTANT SERVICE

Have reasonable expectations of your team, colleagues and peers. Understand that they are busy too, and your request may compete with their other existing priorities.

I have worked with a lot of law firms and professional services firms which can have cultures where instant gratification rules. Partners and associates can have an expectation that their time is expensive and important, therefore their work should be the immediate priority for junior lawyers and support staff. These industries can be very reactive.[29]

No doubt delivering professional services is a competitive business, and the top firms pride themselves on delivering excellent service to their clients. But the age-old culture of instant service that these senior professionals are used to seems unnecessary and outdated to me. My experience is that the urgency created in these firms all too often boils down to a lack of organisation, with work often being left until the last minute. And people get away with it, because they know that there are others who will drop everything to do their bidding whenever they are called upon.

'So what's the problem?', I hear you ask. 'That's what support staff and juniors are for!'

How old school is that? Resources could be so much better employed if the urgency in these firms was dialled down.

Now, it may be a bit harsh of me to single out professional services firms. They may be typically bad at this stuff, but in fact many organisations, no matter the industry, can have a similar culture, though maybe not as extreme.

As a team we should reset our expectations if we do have an instant service expectation. We need to get organised and proactively delegate work or request information in a timely way as much as possible. It's not rocket science!

---

[29] I don't want to pick on professional services firms, but this is a reality that I see all too often.

PART III
Managing Team Urgency

We can learn to be personally more proactive, but what do we actually do about urgency if it's running rampant in our workplace? Managers are often 'the meat in the sandwich' in this regard: they need to deal with pressure from their own direct reporting leader and other members of the leadership team. They also need to manage pressure from below, as their team and others within the organisation push for information, for work to be delivered, for decisions to be made or things to be approved. Add the push and pull from peers and other departments, and managers are dealing with a heap of pressure!

Leaders need to control the tempo of the game. If they don't, someone else will, and that may not be ideal. But, while a good leader involves their management team in the creation of their proactive culture, it is the managers themselves who need to make it happen, and deal with urgency within their team on a day-to-day basis.

If you are not careful, you can easily mismanage urgency, or even become a part of the problem itself. I've worked with many teams on personal productivity where it was obvious that the manager had a highly reactive workstyle; this certainly did not help the team to moderate urgency. Often the manager in question was overwhelmed, and just trying to stay on top of things themselves. This can be especially true with first-time managers, but I find that poor habits learned in these early days can set the tone for their management style well into the future.

As you grow and evolve, gaining valuable experience on the job and from mentors, you may become less reactive to incoming noise and be better able to prioritise and work out what is truly urgent. But you can still retain some poor habits and mindsets around urgency, and drive urgency more than you should.

A well-rounded manager will know how to moderate urgency and use it in a purposeful way to get the right work done at the right time.

You will spot when your team is either caught above the line in the reactive zone or wallowing below the line in the inactive zone. You will know how to turn up the urgency when needed, and turn it down when not. And you will be able to deal with incoming urgency as well as generating internal urgency when required.

Most importantly, you will understand that there is always an opportunity cost if your team is caught up in unproductive urgency. The opportunity cost is work that is not done, or rework that now has to be done. A team like this will always feel busy, and will be busy, but may not be achieving very much. That is a hard road to travel—I'm sure you will agree.

Staying in the active zone

In part I we explored the three zones of urgency (see figure C, overleaf):

1. The active zone is where we are most productive, with a healthy amount of urgency and responsiveness.

2. The reactive zone is where urgency is out of control and causes real problems.

3. The inactive zone is where things slow to a crawl and where we sometimes end up hiding.

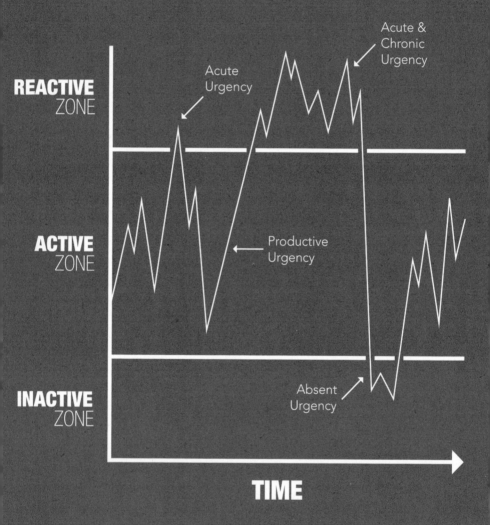

REACTIVE
ZONE

ACTIVE
ZONE

INACTIVE
ZONE

Acute
Urgency

Acute &
Chronic
Urgency

Productive
Urgency

Absent
Urgency

TIME

Figure C: the urgency trap

A manager's role is to keep the team in the active zone as much of the time as possible. They need to turn urgency down when it's unproductive or becoming too much, and they need to turn it up when it's needed to create traction or momentum with critical work. It's a balancing act, but a crucial one as the whole team benefits and should be more able to focus on what is most important more of the time.

The manager's ability to spot when members of the team are creeping up into the reactive zone too much or are stuck in a pattern of chronic urgency can make the difference between a team of healthy workers and a bunch of burnt-out stress balls.

A manager can think of themselves as the driver of the team bus; they have to make constant adjustments to stay in the active zone lane.

These constant adjustments are what I call urgency moderation. In the following chapters, we'll look at the tools you can use to moderate urgency and keep your team working in the right zone.

CHAPTER 6
Moderating urgency

Stephen Covey is probably most famous for his spin on what is often referred to as the Importance/Urgency Matrix. This was a tool developed many years ago to help managers make decisions about where they invest their time. One of the key lessons of this model was the idea of working proactively on the work that was less urgent, but more important. I'm sure you have seen or used this tool at some stage, and I believe it is one of the outstanding pieces of thinking on productivity over the decades.

The matrix outlined in figure 6.1 (overleaf) is a little different to the Covey matrix.[30] I see this as a framework to help both individuals and teams apply a range of strategies to moderate urgency in their workplace. It provides a practical framework for dealing with urgency in any situation, regardless of who is driving the urgency.

The model outlines four key situations in which you may need to moderate urgency, and four key strategies that you can apply to moderate it.

---

[30] This matrix is sometimes referred to as the Eisenhower matrix as US president Eisenhower used it to prioritise his time during his presidency.

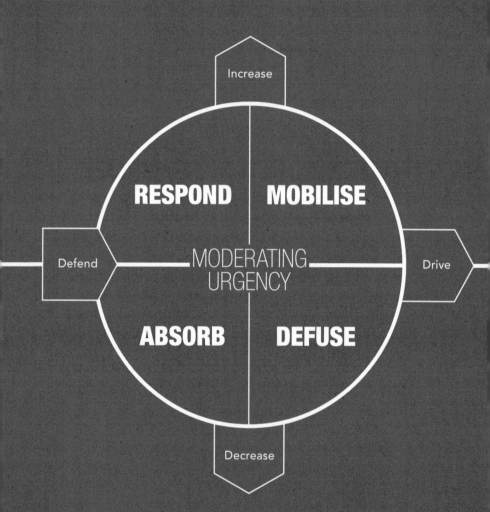

PRODUCTIVE URGENCY

Increase

RESPOND | MOBILISE

Defend — MODERATING URGENCY — Drive

ABSORB | DEFUSE

Decrease

UNPRODUCTIVE URGENCY

Figure 6.1: the urgency matrix

We have discussed how urgency may need to be decreased or increased, depending on whether it's productive or unproductive. This is one of the dynamics we need to consider when evolving our strategies. A second dynamic is whether the urgency is coming at you from others, and therefore needs you to *defend* against it, or whether you actually need to *drive* the urgency in your team.

If we overlay these dynamics on the matrix in figure 6.1, it provides us with strategies we could employ to moderate the urgency. Specifically, we can either Respond or Absorb if we need to defend against the urgency, or we can Mobilise or Defuse if we need to drive the urgency.

1. Respond

You want to increase urgency in the face of externally driven issues or opportunities.

In this situation work has come in, or there is an issue or opportunity that is truly urgent, and you need the team to step up and deal with it in a timely way. This is the stuff that is:

- urgent

- reasonable

- should be dealt with.

The key strategy here is to resist reacting, and to instead *respond* in a measured way. That doesn't mean delaying or putting it off. It simply requires good awareness, a clear head and a measured response.

An example of this might be a report that has been requested by senior management in response to a regulatory investigation. It could not have been planned for, and the expectation is that it be delivered as soon as possible. The organisation must comply and needs a real sense of urgency on the part of all involved. But this should be an unusual situation and would not be the way things get done every day.

2. Absorb

You need to decrease urgency in the face of externally driven busywork.

Here the urgency is not productive and is either not truly urgent or is only urgent because of someone else's poor planning. Remember, a lack of planning on your part should not create a crisis for me. Your role here as a manager is to *absorb* the urgency, and prevent it from causing problems and busywork for your team. This may involve negotiating or at least asking some probing questions. It definitely involves you taking an active stance on unreasonable urgency and empowering your team to do the same.

A good example of this might be one of many requests that come into a back-office support team every day. Every request is urgent and each person thinks that their issue is the most critical and should be dealt with immediately. But you know the work is not truly urgent or is only urgent because the other team did not plan it well.

3. Mobilise

You want to increase urgency within your team to create traction or momentum.

Sometimes you need to drive the urgency yourself to get traction or build momentum with a priority or a project. This urgency is being driven from within and requires you to *mobilise* the troops. But this strategy needs to be used with care and requires you to be purposeful and clear in your communication. Many people talk about the idea of creating a 'burning platform' to mobilise teams, and we often say we need to 'light a fire under' someone to get them moving. This is hot mobilisation language!

Mobilisation happens from within the team, in situations where the manager has identified projects or opportunities that need focus and traction in order to meet the team's goals and objectives. It is the manager's job to mobilise the team behind these initiatives.

4. Defuse

You want to decrease unproductive urgency being created within the team.

In some situations, you may need to *defuse* urgency within your own team, and drive the urgency down. If you need to light a fire under people to mobilise them, here you need to throw a bucket of water on the urgency![31] When you spot unproductive reactive behaviours being consistently demonstrated by your team, you may need to step in and take control. Like letting some air out of an overinflated balloon, you need to take the pressure out of the situation and get the team refocused on the real priorities.

An example of this might be members of a team who are so used to dealing with urgent requests from the wider business that they make everything urgent. It's the only way they know; in

---

[31] This reminds me of a dogfight on my street when I was a kid. Two dogs were ripping into each other, with a crowd of bystanders looking on, but not acting to break it up. Finally a neighbour came out and threw a bucket of cold water on the dogs. Fight over!

fact, sometimes it's how they feel good about themselves. They equate being productive with being busy in reactive mode.

————

We can apply these four strategies in a practical way in our day-to-day situations.

In the next chapters, we explore each strategy in detail and look at a range of practical ways that you as a manager can use to moderate urgency for your team.

URGENCY PLAYBOOK
<u>PRINCIPLE 6</u>

USE APPROPRIATE TOOLS FOR URGENT REQUESTS

Avoid using tools such as email as the only way to communicate urgent requests. Agree on the most appropriate methods to communicate real urgency within your team.

When all you have is a hammer, everything looks like a nail. And email is a hammer that we all use too much, especially for urgent issues. In my workshops I often ask people only check their emails once every hour. This causes great consternation as many people feel that they will miss urgent emails if they do not see the email the minute it comes in. It is a crazy but very real fear.

This would not be such an issue if we agreed as a team not to use inappropriate tools such as email to communicate urgent issues. We simply get too many emails for this to be an effective channel for truly urgent communications. If you sit down as a team and discuss the best ways to communicate urgency, you can then create a team agreement that will get everyone working in a more productive way. And real urgency is more likely to be noticed and acted upon.

CHAPTER 7
Respond

In this chapter we'll talk about the *respond* quadrant of the urgency matrix (see figure 7.1, overleaf).

Sometimes things come at you that are urgent and could not have been planned for. That is life, and no amount of planning or anticipation can stop this: our work is complex and we are dealing with many different people, projects, time zones and locations. The key is not to eradicate urgency altogether, but to make it the exception rather than the rule. To make it 20 per cent of our time, rather than 80 per cent. But even if something is truly urgent, I counsel you to learn to respond quickly rather than react instantly, except in the most critical of situations. (Take this advice with a good pinch of common sense. If you are about to be hit by a car — jump out of the way quickly!)

A friend and colleague of mine is a film director and advertising guru. Simon 'Mo' Macrae, or Mo to his friends, tells a great story in his classes on creativity and video content. He recounts a piece of advice a business mentor gave him. The advice was 'when you are faced with an amazing contract, PUT DOWN THE PEN'. In other words, before signing your life away, put down the pen so that you have a moment to think about what this really means for you. What are the benefits? What are the pitfalls? What is the opportunity cost?

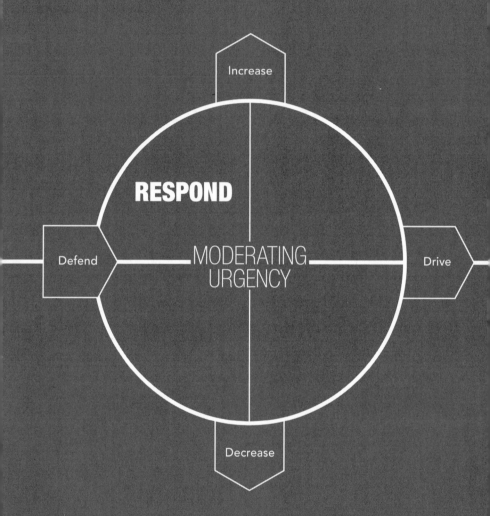

Figure 7.1: the urgency matrix: respond

This became Mo's way of stopping himself from signing contracts without really thinking about them first. A great circuit breaker, don't you think? This idea is the key to becoming more responsive and less reactive.

Because so much of our work is driven by emails and other 'instant' communication tools, we now operate in a business environment where it's all too easy to fall into the trap of mindlessly reacting to inputs. I see many people who fall into the trap of equating providing instant responses to high productivity. They have a reactive workstyle that is driven by urgency. But this is rarely productive in the long run, as there is an opportunity cost: more important priorities get dropped to deal with all of the urgent reactive issues.

A challenge can be that many workers in the modern email-driven workplace feel they get measured on the speed at which they react to these inputs. And unfortunately, they often are.[32]

The key to working effectively when dealing with incoming work is to have a bias for responsiveness rather than reactivity.

So, what's the difference? I reckon having a responsive approach to our work signifies a more balanced, timely and thoughtful approach to incoming work. It's about being importance-driven vs urgency-driven. When we are responsive, we put the pen down and think for a moment before signing.

---

[32] I often think it is ironic that email, once hailed as the fastest way to communicate because it was instant, has now become the slowest way to communicate in some organisations as it can take so long for busy managers to get to them.

The urge to react is in our DNA, from the days when we were cave dwellers. Fight or flight is what we were designed to do. Quick reactions were critical when hunting, and running from predators. But for most of us today, in most situations, our world is not that risky. Now that we've taken off the loincloths and put on the business suits, we need a more measured approach to work.

Our worlds are much more complex and contain way too many inputs to allow reactivity to rule. In the face of such information overload and complexity, we need to take control again so we remain firmly focused on what is important in our roles. A responsive approach to work puts your priorities centre-stage, rather than getting caught up in less meaningful work.

Reactive versus responsive

Figure 7.2 is a good summary of the subtle differences between reactivity and responsiveness.

Urgency vs importance

When we work reactively, we tend to prioritise our work according to how urgent it is. People who are responsive tend to put importance before urgency, or at least consider both before responding.[33] This leads to more *important* work getting done rather than just more work getting done. I believe this is the real difference between highly productive people and people who are simply well organised.

The well-organised person gets a lot done, but the highly productive person ensures they identify the right stuff first, then strives to get as much of that done in the time available.

---

[33] Remember we discussed criticality on page 79?

REACTIVE	RESPONSIVE
Urgency driven	Importance driven
Knee-jerk	Measured
Instinctive	Deliberate
Half-baked decisions	Healthy decisions
Risk-prone	Risk-managed
Mindlessly disrupts plans	Thoughtfully adjusts plans
Stressful	Calm
Unproductive	Productive

Figure 7.2: reactive versus responsive

Knee-jerk vs measured

We often use the term 'knee-jerk reaction' to describe an instinctive reaction to something. The knee-jerk response happens automatically *without the brain being involved*. Likewise, knee-jerk reactions are not thought through, and may not involve your brain either. When we are responsive we tend to be more measured in our approach, and think clearly about the best course of action.

Instinctive vs deliberate

Similarly, when we simply react we are probably relying on our instincts rather than being deliberate in our actions. This is fine in some situations, like when we're about to be hit by a car, but if it's the rule rather than the exception, we risk becoming unproductively reactive.

Half-baked vs healthy decisions

Reactivity, and the half-baked decisions that often result from it, increases the risk of mistakes and rework down the track. That said, there is research that shows that leaders who make fast decisions are more effective than those who deliberate for too long. But fast does not have to mean instant. This research is talking about the effectiveness of being responsive in decision making rather than procrastinating.

Risk-prone vs risk-managed

Responsiveness can definitely manage or reduce risk in your role. But I often wonder how many costly mistakes are made in organisations because everyone is running at a hundred miles an hour all of the time.

Mindless disruptions vs thoughtful adjustments

When we react, the resultant interruption can disrupt our existing work, and even our whole day. When we respond, we tend to measure the new work against our existing work, and make a prioritised decision. Our new work becomes a part of an updated plan rather than exploding the plan.

Stress vs calm

There is no doubt that working reactively is more stressful than working responsively. Being responsive forces us to take control of what is happening. Yet there is a calmness that comes with taking the responsive approach that I personally cherish.

Unproductive vs productive

Finally, I would strongly argue that when we are being reactive we are at risk of being unproductive; when we are working in a responsive way, we are more likely to be working productively. I believe that all of these factors add up to a decrease in overall productivity when we react, and an increase in overall productivity when we respond.

But how do we break the habit of reacting, which for many of us is so ingrained, driven by the reactive environments we work in?

Create a circuit breaker

The phrase 'a knee-jerk reaction' was first coined by Sir Michael Foster in 1877, in his book *Textbook of Physiology*. Originally it was a medical term used to describe the body's reaction when the tendon below the knee is struck with an object, causing the leg to extend automatically, without the signal passing through the brain. In the early 1900s it started to be used as a term that described reactivity.

In today's busy workplaces, I believe that the tendon below our figurative knee is being repeatedly hit with a hammer, and we are conditioned to just react *every time*. As discussed in part I, the pace of business over the past few decades has increased enormously, but for what reason? Are we dealing with more important issues today than in the 1970s? Has the fundamental nature of doing business changed so much in that time? I don't believe so. All that has happened is that communication has become more instant and more voluminous, and we have come to accept this as normal.

But this is a problem of our own making. In a study called 'Evaluating the effect of email interruptions within the workplace', the researchers found that emails within a research group were, on average, attended to within six seconds of arrival. This might be okay in a fire department or ambulance service, but surely not in usual, everyday businesses, such as a bank, a marketing organisation, a manufacturing company or a consultancy firm.

If you were more responsive and less reactive, you might actually get more done.

Remember, our bodies and brains have been wired to react over millions of years. We need to learn to override our instinctive reactions and create the space to respond. We need a circuit breaker to find the space that lives between reaction and response.

The space between reaction and response

Many rugby union fans complain about the increasing number of rules and penalties slowing the game down too much. But rugby employs these measures to reduce the risk of injury, which seems eminently sensible to me. For example, scrums in rugby are terribly dangerous situations, with two groups of heavy men or women binding together, arm around shoulder, and then charging headfirst into each other. A typical forward line of rugby players would weigh between 800 and 900 kilos in total, and they are the ones who make up the scrum. Two sets of 900 kilos slamming into each other—not my cup of tea.[34]

There is a real risk of neck injury, especially for the players in the front row, who directly contact the other team. If not executed properly, the scrum can also collapse, again risking injury to the players.

To manage this, the International Rugby Board have trialled different techniques the referee can use to slow things down a bit and get the players to focus on good technique. The current strategy is for the ref to call 'Crouch, bind, set' to direct the players. When they call 'Crouch' the players get into position, grabbing on to their teammates. When they call 'Bind' they then grab hold of the opposing forwards, and when they call 'Set' they crash into each other.[35]

If it works well, nobody gets injured and one of the teams gets the ball while the scrum untangle themselves from the resultant pile. I believe that is the advantage gained and the whole point of this weird sporting ritual. During the scrum, the directions from the ref serve as a circuit breaker and encourage the players to focus and think about what they are doing. It's not perfect, but it does help.

---

[34] I did go to a rugby school in Dublin but opted for the squash team after one game. I was a skinny little thing!

[35] Crazy stuff, but if you love rugby, it is one of the highlights or lowlights of the game, depending on your preferences. If you don't love rugby, I'm sure you are a bit bewildered.

We can employ a similar strategy if we want to avoid reacting to incoming work, and instead respond in a more thoughtful way. When we react to incoming work, we might not risk an injury to ourselves or our colleagues, but we do risk an injury to our existing priorities. There is a sacred space between response and reaction, which is full of promise and opportunity if we stop for a minute to see it.

Four things happen if we stop and move from reactive to responsive mode, as shown in figure 7.3:

1. **Pause**: We recognise this as a moment of possible reaction.

2. **Evaluate**: We reflect and try to understand what the request/issue/communication is about, what is required and why it is relevant to us.

3. **Prioritise**: We consider the opportunity cost to us if we switch activities and decide if the new incoming work is more important than our current work.

4. **Decide**: We decide on the best course of action. Whatever decision we make will result in a response, but the response could be to deal with the new issue immediately, push back and negotiate, or to ignore it entirely for the moment.

It's not easy to shift our mindset if we are very reactive, but with patience and practice, it can be done. Often what we need is something or someone that will serve as a circuit breaker. This is what the referee does in the rugby scrum.

One of my mates has a habit of removing people from the To and CC fields in an email response as this forces him to review the email before he presses send. It also forces him to be more mindful about who he addresses the response to.

REACTION [PAUSE EVALUATE PRIORITISE DECIDE] RESPONSE

Figure 7.3: the space between reaction and response

So, look out for that moment of reaction. When you spot it you get to choose: Do I react as I have always done, or do I take a moment to respond appropriately?

James MacNevin, the head of Asia Pacific for State Street Global Advisors, has a clear approach to urgent requests:

> I sense that everyone is so time poor, that if you classified something as non-urgent, 'take your time to respond', the fear is that it will never be actioned. I've tried a few techniques in terms of dealing with this issue. Firstly, I make it clear that the quality of my response is often dictated by how much time I have to consider the issue. If you want an answer now, it may be NO, unless you put the work in to explain.
>
> I try and triage issues:
>
> • how time critical the issue is; do you require an answer now, next two hours, next two days …
>
> • how complex the issue is; will this require detailed analysis considering multiple options, or is it a yes/no decision …
>
> • does the issue impact a client?
>
> I'm often okay to respond to non-complex issues fairly quickly, even if these are not super critical. I think it's important to keep the wheels spinning, as it were, and as we're a reasonably flat organization, I like to make decisions quickly if it's a simple yes/no matter.
>
> For urgent matters that are more complex, I want the individual to have at least put some work into the matter that will make decision-making effective. I try to force a simple construct:
>
> 1. describe the issue/business context
>
> 2. state our options
>
> 3. suggest the preferred option and rationale.
>
> I will make quicker and better decisions when I'm properly briefed. My experience is that most issues that are presented to me as urgent are not actually that pressing. In fact, it's often

the case that items that do warrant immediate attention are not properly presented to get that required real time response.

So, James, as a senior executive, is saying that the easier you make it for him, the quicker he will make it for you. That seems like a reasonable deal. ASAP does not cut it with him. He expects more of his people, but will respond quickly if they have done the work to deserve his fast response.

How will you look to change your reactions into responses? Maybe printing out the model in figure 7.3[36] and putting it on your desk might serve as a good reminder for you. Or maybe you can come up with a phrase or motto that you repeat to yourself when new work comes in, something that will cut through and force you to stop for a moment.

This is such a good skill to develop in your team. It's not a hard thing to teach, and can become one of the agreed behaviours that contribute to your team culture.

Test assumptions

Just because something looks urgent does not mean it is. I am reminded of a scene in *Apollo 13*, where an alarm goes off in the cockpit, and Tom Hanks, playing the spacecraft commander, says 'Houston, is this something we should be concerned about?' Ground control checked it out and replied that no, they could ignore that alarm.

One of the benefits of pausing for a moment before reacting is that it allows you to test assumptions. There is a risk that if we react blindly, we are assuming that the work is urgent, and not considering the option of negotiating.

---

[36] You can download at www.urgentbook.com.

I recently bought a new house, and have been going through all of the ups and downs associated with one of the biggest events of your life. This was a classic case of hurry up and wait. In a flurry of urgent activity we finalised the sale with the vendor, and then supplied all of the information to our bank to finalise the loan. Then it was wait, wait, wait. Finally, we got the call to say it was all approved, and then it was all go, go, go!

We received an email on a Friday from the bank saying that we needed to come in and sign the loan documents. All good, except that my partner was flying to Singapore for work on the following Monday. She called me to raise this issue, and was hoping I could reschedule my Friday afternoon to go into the bank to sign immediately. My instinct was to react and drive into the bank. But I forced myself to test some assumptions. On rereading the email, I noticed that the loan documents would not be ready for 48 hours, so we couldn't sign that day anyway.

A phone call later and plan B was in place, and we could relax. Because our emotions and stress levels were high, we almost reacted and wasted time in our panic. Not a big deal in the scheme of things, but these are all the little things that can drag our productivity down when we are working. And it can feel like death by a thousand cuts.

In a reactive situation where we assume something to be urgent, we sometimes miss the cues that would suggest that it is not.

There are two sets of assumptions you need to test:

1. your own

2. those of the originator.

Firstly, test *your own assumptions* about the urgency involved. I see many people react to incoming work, assuming that the requests are urgent. But upon investigation, the originator would indicate that it was not that urgent in reality. Of course, the other person is happy to get it quickly, but they may not have requested a fast turnaround.

We often assume urgency if the work is coming from above. Ideally others will indicate clearly when something is required, but when we are all so busy, this often gets missed. People don't clearly state their expectations, so we end up making erroneous assumptions. If a request comes in without a clear deadline or date expected, go back and clarify when it is needed by. Do this consistently and people will begin to communicate these things to you proactively. Try not to leave a meeting with any actions that do not have a clear due date. When you take on the work you take on the responsibility of managing it in a timely way. As a manager, you may need to coach your team to do this.

Secondly, *test their assumptions* about the urgency of the work. They might be making their own assumptions about how urgent something is, but your knowledge or experience could help to reset their expectations.

I know to some this may sound like it is going to create a lot more back and forth communications, and that will waste time. But the wasted time spent on reacting blindly is more costly, in my book.[37]

The language of urgency

'When do you need that by'?

'ASAP.'

---

[37] Literally in my book. In fact, in all three of my books if I think about it.

In project management circles the terms ASAP (as soon as possible) and ALAP (as late as possible) are common terms. In a project, ASAP is a way to schedule work so that it builds a buffer at the back end of the project if there are overruns or delays. Project managers use scheduling software to work out the earliest possible date a task could be done, depending on the other tasks that must be completed before the task can start. That makes sense (I think).

But how does ALAP fit in? Why would we want to be leaving things until as late as possible, especially in a project context? Well, usually for budgeting purposes. When large amounts of money are being spent in a project, cash flow can have a real impact. Why pay $500000 now when the task could be delayed by three months without having a material impact on the project deadline? There may also be circumstances where ASAP or ALAP can help resolve resourcing conflicts as well.

However, outside of the world of projects, 'ASAP' has become a common cry for 'urgent'! 'I need this ASAP!', 'The boss wants us in her office ASAP', 'Let's get this done ASAP'. Many email subject lines will include these capitalised letters just to be sure. Yet, you rarely (if ever) hear the term 'ALAP' being used. How refreshing would it be to hear a manager delegate a piece of work and ask for it to be on their desk as late as possible! I fear that this language is a part of the urgency problem.

I believe there is a third option available to us that opens up a more positive pathway to urgency: ASAR, which stands for *as soon as reasonable*.

In my mind, as soon as *possible* suggests that you shift existing priorities to get this done now. This new work takes priority and you need to make it happen quickly. But as soon as *reasonable* suggests you blend the work in with your other priorities rather than pushing the new priority in front of all the others. It's similar to merging two lanes of traffic into one like the two strands of a zipper coming together in an orderly fashion. ASAP is more like cars just pushing in aggressively, without any order.

Terms such as ASAP and ASAR can set the tone for how a team deals with urgency. Language is very powerful, and if ASAP is what people hear more often than not, it creates a culture of urgency. But managers have the opportunity to introduce a new language that provides a more positive approach to urgency.

Maybe it's worth having a talk to your team about these acronyms, and how they could be used to provide a fairer and more balanced indication of what is expected when work is requested from others — or even from you.

React when required

Of course, there will always be some situations that require an instant reaction. We will never get rid of this urgency; we just aim to minimise it. But when something truly urgent comes your way, you need to drop everything and deal with it.

One of the advantages of working more proactively as a rule is that it gives you more flexibility to react when you need to. There is less risk that other urgent deadlines are going to be affected if something pops up. Other people are more forgiving if you need to reschedule a meeting at the last minute, as they know this is not your normal modus operandi. And your team are more likely to step up to help you if you have not cried wolf many times before.

If your team need to react to something out of the blue, it's important to adjust the team's priorities so that everything does not just fall into a heap. Is there work that could be transferred to another part of the team, or to another team altogether to keep it moving? Do you need to communicate with stakeholders to inform them that their work may need to be delayed due to this change? Are there meetings in your schedule that need to be cleared, and could you give the meeting organisers a heads up sooner rather than later?

You see, even in a reactive moment there are proactive things you can do that will make life easier for you and others.

The strategies outlined here are designed to help you to meet urgency in a reasonable way. Responding is a defensive strategy to deal with reasonable urgency. Next, we will explore another defensive strategy that can be used when urgency is unreasonable.

URGENCY PLAYBOOK
<u>PRINCIPLE 7</u>

BE RESPONSIVE, NOT REACTIVE

Don't just react to incoming work and information. Check incoming work regularly but not constantly, and, when necessary, respond in a timely way.

As we have already discussed, there is a big difference between being responsive and being reactive. Responsiveness is a more deliberate, purposeful and considered response to something, rather than an instinctive reaction.

Of course, we need to be reactive sometimes, when something is truly urgent and the impact of inaction would be severe. When a colleague falls down the stairs, please react and get help as soon as possible! But in our normal work context, being responsive is about dialling down the urgency and ensuring your response is measured and appropriate.

As a team, it's worth considering the difference between responsiveness and reactivity, and agreeing to become more responsive with each other and less reactive. This also includes becoming more responsive to things that you might currently procrastinate and leave in the pile for too long. The funny thing you will find is that if you stop procrastinating and become more responsive, a lot of the unnecessary urgency that we create disappears.

CHAPTER 8
Absorb

Now on to the *absorb* quadrant of the urgency matrix (see figure 8.1, overleaf).

Remember, a manager's responsibility to their team is to protect them from unnecessary urgency. A part of that role is to act as a shock absorber or buffer that will dampen the urgency being driven by other parts of the organisation — from stakeholders, from senior management and from clients.

This is a contentious idea, as many see the manager's role as a conductor of that urgency. That you should be communicating the urgency to your team, and ensuring they get on with the job with a sense of urgency. But I see this leading more often than not to *senseless* urgency, rather than a *sense of* urgency. And remember, in many cases the urgency is neither real nor reasonable.

Your job is to evaluate the request and work out if the urgency is real or not, and if it is reasonable or not.

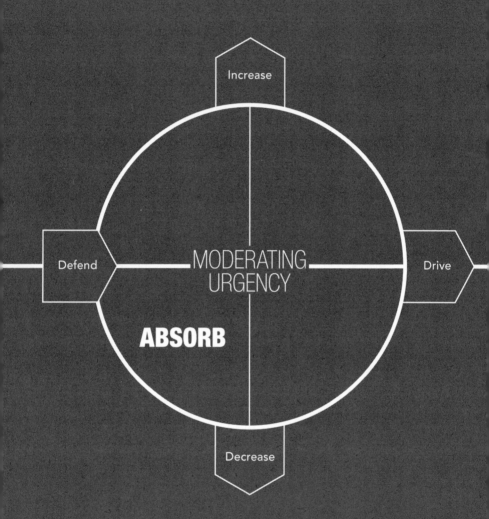

PRODUCTIVE URGENCY

Increase

Defend

MODERATING
URGENCY

Drive

ABSORB

Decrease

UNPRODUCTIVE URGENCY

Figure 8.1: the urgency matrix: absorb

One manager I worked with was definitely an urgency conductor. Many requests and issues came his way from the leadership team in the organisation. He invariably passed these urgent crises straight to his team, pulling them off whatever they were working on. His team were in a constant state of anxiety, and felt that they could never plan as their week or day was always rearranged at the last moment. But they did not feel that many of these issues were truly urgent. They felt that other more senior managers made things urgent either because that was how they got stuff done, or they left things until the last minute and then made the request. Their manager did not manage this well and expected the team to suck it up. Not surprisingly this was a high stress, high turnover team.

So, what can you do to absorb the urgency a bit?

Question why

The first thing you can do is develop the healthy habit of questioning why. Why is this urgent? Is it really urgent at all? Rather than divert your team to the issue immediately, force the other party to justify the urgency. If they can, all good. But if not, maybe your team should not be distracted by the issue at all.

One of my clients shared a story about how she had dealt with an urgent meeting request that would involve herself and three of her team. The request came through to schedule a meeting for the next day to discuss an urgent issue. There was no detail or agenda provided with the request. The manager calmly sent a response saying that if she and her team were to come to a last-minute meeting, she would require a full overview of the issue, stating why it was so urgent, with a proper agenda attached and sent through that day for her to review. Funnily enough, the meeting organiser never responded, and the meeting never went ahead. At least not with her team in it.

So, don't just accept urgency for your team. Question it consistently.

If you do this in a firm and polite way, people will not experience you as hard to work with. They will see you as someone who is focused on what is important and someone who will not suffer their time being wasted. Set the expectation that you do not accept urgent issues derailing the important work of your team without very good reason, even if it does come from above. As a manager, your ability to manage upwards is critical here.

Negotiate

While the urgency dials (covered in chapter 5) can be used to negotiate urgency at a personal workload management level, guess what? This is also the perfect tool to negotiate urgency at the team level.

In order to negotiate effectively, you need to be aware of the demands placed on your team. This requires visibility of their priorities. This is a tricky one, as you don't want to become a micro-manager or to become the bottleneck that every request must pass through. I always find the best solution is to create visibility across the team is to ensure that there is an agreed central place where all major priorities are captured and recorded for the team.

The challenge in most teams is that priorities are often managed in an invisible way.

When we discussed how to work proactively, I highlighted the fact that we often capture things in a list, or in an Excel spreadsheet, or in our inbox or, worst of all, in our head. But these places are invisible to our manager and the rest of our team. And when the work is invisible, it's hard to manage resourcing issues or unreasonable urgency being placed on the team.

Many teams are now starting to use web-based project tools to make key priorities visible across the whole team.[38] These simple interfaces allow the team to make key priorities visible, along with key information such as deadlines, assignment, progress and sub-tasks. These tools can be used for project work as well as standalone priorities, but are best used for bigger chunks of work rather than smaller individual tasks.

The value of these tools is that anyone in the team can easily see what is on their own plate and on other people's plates, at any one time. As a manager, this gives you a dashboard to see what is happening, and to have open conversations with your team about the deadlines they are facing, and the negotiation that might need to happen if some of those deadlines have been pushed on your team in an unreasonable way.

Of course, you may need to jump into a negotiation on behalf of a team member as the request comes in. Waiting for your weekly team meeting may be too late. So your team may need to know when they need to escalate something to you as it comes in. You don't want them to have to check with you on every detail, so it's worth having a conversation with them and coaching them on what they should be able to negotiate themselves, and when it may need to be escalated.

---

[38] At the time of writing, some popular tools in use for this are MS Planner, Trello, Asana and Jira.

Oh, and by the way, make sure you deliver as promised if you do negotiate a change to a deadline! There is nothing worse than negotiating in good faith and then letting them down anyway.

Back your team

One of my good mates, Charles, is a senior manager with one of the big banks. Charles and I have a weekend away each year with a group of friends where we play poker and golf, and drink way too much whisky and wine.

This year, Charles and I decided it was no use pretending that we actually enjoyed golf. We did not and it showed. So, we waved goodbye to the boys for a few hours and instead walked the Bouddi Track in NSW. This is a pleasant coastal track that takes a few hours to walk in the hot sun, and allows for great conversation.

I was keen to get Charles's input on my thinking for this book, as he had many years' experience working in some very large organisations. The greatest gem that I got from him that day was that he always backed his team.

His team did some high-level financial analysis for parts of the bank, and often for very senior managers and leaders. You would imagine they got a lot of urgent requests from above. He coached his team to deliver excellent service to their stakeholders, but Charles told me that he worried if he was not getting enough complaints from the business about his team. That stopped me in my tracks.[39]

He said he expected a reasonable number of complaints about his team from the business as they were saying no to, or pushing

---

[39] Or *on the* track, as it were.

back on, urgent requests. His logic was this: he empowered his team to make good decisions about what was urgent or important. If he was not getting complaints from the business, that was a sign they were not prioritising properly. And if he did get complaints, he listened patiently, but he invariably backed his team. He did not receive the complaint and then admonish his team member. He stood up for them and told the business he supported them, and to his mind they had made the right decision. That said, I am sure if his team member was in the wrong, he would own that too.

Charles is a fair person. He treats his team fairly. He treats the business fairly. But he does not tolerate unreasonable urgency, or unreasonable colleagues who just want everything now.

How about you? Do you back your team or do you cave in a little too easily to the cries from the business?

Identify the bigger YES

The truth is that time is our most limited resource, and we have way more to do than we have time available. So, whenever we have our head stuck in our inbox, that is time we are not spending on something potentially more important. The same is true of meetings. Every time you're in a meeting thinking 'What has this got to do with my role?', that is time you could have spent on something more critical to your goals and objectives.

Every time you say *yes* to something you should have said *no* to, you are also saying *no* to something you should be saying *yes* to.

Wise words indeed, even if they are a bit of a mind bender. So, if you need to refocus effort, it can be useful to get your team to reconnect with the bigger YES that they should be working on, rather than getting themselves distracted by this urgent activity.

Where do they go to find this bigger YES? Their performance plan, goals and objectives document or quarterly plan might be a good place to start.

I often find that people may have these documents, which clearly outline what they should be focused on and achieving in their role. They may think they know what's in them but can often find themselves disconnected from them. If they were to hold up these plans and then look at their schedule and task list, they might find there is a bit of a mismatch. The busy activity in their schedule is often not the right activity to achieve what they will get measured on.

At the start of each month I outline my top 10 priorities for the month. I review the BIG picture — my goals and objectives, my projects and my outcomes, and I ask myself, 'What are the 10 things that I want to move forward over the next month?' This list usually ends up with a mix of work and personal priorities that will move me towards my objectives. Our friend Stephen Covey called this type of priority the 'Big Rocks'. This concept, outlined in *First Things First* and *The Seven Habits of Highly Effective People*, has been well documented over the years, and has become a part of the common vernacular in many organisations.

We all know what 'Big Rocks' refer to, but few of us drive them into our schedule well enough. We hold the rocks in our head and instead get busy with urgent emails, meetings and issues that may make us feel productive, but actually get in the way of the real priorities.

So, if you want to refocus your team's effort, do this:

- Get them to sit down for half an hour and list down what they consider to be their top 10 important priorities for the next month.

- Have a conversation with them about their list and provide your input if necessary.

- Make sure they schedule next-step actions into their planning systems to move the needle on these rocks.

Another angle is to consider if the incoming urgency is on what they call the 'critical path'. In project terms, the critical path is the shortest path of activities in a project plan, which signifies the shortest possible time the project could be completed in. Anything that is delayed on the critical path runs the risk of delaying the project deadline. Anything not on the critical path has more flexibility. Knowing this sort of information is really useful when you are trying to help your team prioritise.

When you are clear about what is important, it makes it much easier to evaluate incoming urgent work and make good decisions about what to do with it. Having a clear set of priorities, and a clear plan, makes decision-making much easier.

I sometimes use an analogy about personal values: when you have defined a clear set of personal values, it makes it easier to make decisions about what you feel is right versus wrong.

Likewise, having a clear set of priorities makes it easier to decide what's important and what's merely urgent.

Ignore it if you can

What, ignore it you say? I have to be very careful here, but let me pass on wisdom that many senior managers have shared with me over the years. With many seemingly urgent issues, if you ignore them for 24 hours or so, they miraculously resolve themselves and do not require your intervention at all. How good is that?

———

Having looked at some strategies that can help you and your team defend against urgency coming at you from external sources, it's time now to look at how we can increase or drive urgency from within. How do we get traction with important initiatives and projects, and how can we spot and deal with unproductive reactive behaviours that have developed within our own team?

URGENCY PLAYBOOK
<u>PRINCIPLE 8</u>

MINIMISE DISTRACTION WHEN INTERRUPTING OTHERS

Don't interrupt your colleagues every time you think of something. Be mindful and purposeful with your interruptions so that you reduce the distraction for them.

One of the common complaints I hear when running workshops is about the number of physical interruptions people get, especially in open-plan or activity-based workspaces. I myself encourage people to get out from behind their keyboard and to talk to others more, as I feel we are losing the informal collaboration that can be so productive because of the prevalence of email.

But that does not mean I want you to interrupt someone every time you think of something to discuss. Many interruptions are to discuss things that could have waited until another time. But often you think of a question when you see someone, and you don't have another way to capture and remember it, so you interrupt them immediately. This means you are making the interruption urgent even though it probably is not time critical.

We need strategies to capture discussion items for our team and colleagues, and we need times when we can discuss these things in a more productive, less interruptive way.

Again, mindfulness and purposefulness come into play here.

CHAPTER 9
Mobilise

Now we move to the *mobilise* quadrant of the urgency matrix (see figure 9.1, overleaf).

In the last chapter we talked about defending against urgency that's coming at you from external sources, whether they're outside of your organisation or from other departments or teams within your organisation. What about when the urgency needs to be internally driven? What do you need to do to create a sense of urgency within your own team?

Not all urgency is driven from outside your team. Sometimes you're the one who needs to create the urgency or a sense of it. This may be especially true with projects that have longer time frames than normal day-to-day work. It's so easy for people to work on a new project and feel that they have plenty of time because the delivery date is six months away. The risk is if they are not mobilised early then time will pass and suddenly there is a mountain of work to be done at the back end.

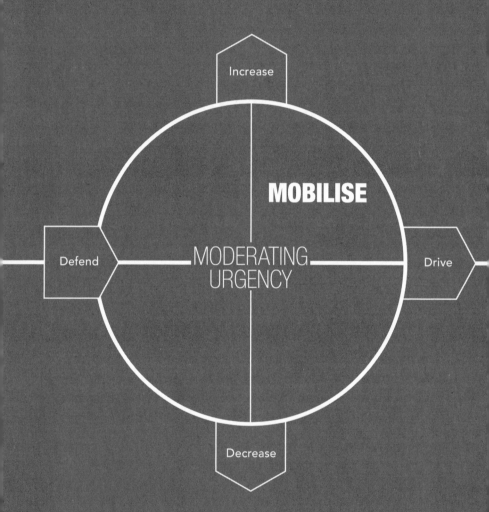

PRODUCTIVE URGENCY

Increase

MOBILISE

Defend

MODERATING
URGENCY

Drive

Decrease

UNPRODUCTIVE URGENCY

Figure 9.1: the urgency matrix: mobilise

So in this scenario, a manager needs to mobilise the troops and keep them moving forward in a steady but progressive way so that the project builds traction and momentum. One of the challenges you may have with this is being too busy yourself to focus on mobilisation; the strategies outlined below take time. John Kotter suggests in his book *A Sense of Urgency* that one of the key enemies of urgency is a crowded schedule. If you are caught in a cycle of endless meetings you may not have the space or the flexibility to have the quick chats, the gentle prods or the key conversations that can keep things on track. As a manager, your role should be less about doing and more about helping others to do, so make sure you protect time in your schedule for this.

Set accountable deadlines

The word 'deadline' has an interesting history. Originally it was used to describe a line about 6 metres outside of a stockade at Andersonville during the American Civil War. Any prisoner who stepped across this line could be shot dead on sight.[40]

Over time the word came to represent any line that should not be crossed. (You may not be shot dead, but it does imply some serious trouble!) In the newspaper business it also came to represent a space on a page where the print would not print properly.

Finally, it came to be most associated with describing a time constraint when, again in the newspaper business, it described the latest time an article could be submitted before that day's paper went to press. Now the word 'deadline' is ubiquitous and is used daily in our workplaces. 'I have a major deadline looming', 'Let's make sure we don't miss the deadline' and 'The

---

[40] I mention this in *Smart Teams* as well, but think it's such a cool word origin it is worth mentioning again.

deadline is the end of the month' would all be familiar phrases to most of us.

Deadlines can be 'hard', meaning they are non-negotiable, or 'soft', meaning they are aspirational but could move if required. Either way they can be a useful tool in some situations.

An example of this is in the housing market, where auctions are a tool used by real estate agents to create a sense of urgency and force people to move quickly. An auction basically sets a deadline for when the house will be sold, so you need to be prepared to buy on that date if not before.

As I've mentioned, I recently bought a new house with my partner, Vera. After months of looking at show houses and scouring the internet for new listings, we finally found the house we loved and were in a position to move on it.

This is the funny thing when entering the housing market. There can be a long period of looking at things, but not being quite ready to buy, either for emotional or financial reasons. This means that if you see a house you like, you may not be ready to move quickly. This happened to us and we missed out on a house that we liked but were just not ready to bid on.

This forced us to get all of our ducks in a row and get ourselves properly prepared to make an offer. Soon after, a house came up that was perfect. We could afford it. We were ready. But we knew that it would go quickly, so we had to mobilise and move quickly. So, after an inspection, we put in an offer. A flurry of activity followed and, after a bit of haggling, our offer was accepted. Happy days. But then 'hurry up and wait' kicked in and things slowed down.

We had signed the contract and paid a deposit, only to find out that the vendor had to go interstate suddenly and was not available to sign his side of the contract. Don't worry, we were told; it should be signed tomorrow. Then the next day. Then the next day! We were getting worried and felt that we were in a very vulnerable position. Unfortunately, there was little we could do, except chase the agent every day and huff and puff.

I then realised that the vendor had all of the power in this situation, so I decided to use our own deadline to mobilise him into action. I told the agent on the Monday morning that this situation was not okay, and our expectation was that the contract would be fully signed by 5 pm, otherwise we would withdraw the offer.

It may have been coincidence, but two hours later I received a text to say that the vendor would be signing that afternoon. Funny that. It's easy to drag our heels when there is no consequence, but as soon as there are ramifications, we treat things with the urgency they deserve, as they say.

Deadlines are a good way to mobilise and to get traction, but they need to be used with purpose and only when needed.

False deadlines or too many deadlines just push people into the *reactive* zone and can have a negative impact. So, use them for good, not for evil! When we do set deadlines for people, I think it's important to be specific about the required date (and sometimes the exact time of day) and to enforce the deadline. Don't let it pass without comment. People will see you as an easy mark and know that you don't really mean your deadlines.

A culture of accountability

Managing deadline expectations is really about managing accountability. I am often asked the question, 'How do I make my team more accountable?' Work is delegated but then seems to fall into a hole unless you chase it up regularly. Many managers find the issue is not so much with intentions — most of us have good intentions when we are given the work. The big issue is overwhelm. We are simply overwhelmed by the volume of things we need to do. And if nobody holds us accountable, we guiltily let things slip through the cracks.

When managing deadlines, you must create a culture of accountability within the team. This can be done in two ways.

Firstly, make it clear that if you say Friday, you mean Friday. Don't allow your team to creep past the deadline unnoticed. This means you need a good system in place to remember everything you have asked people to do and when the deadlines are. I personally keep a list of delegated work and deadlines on a page in MS OneNote for each of my team. And I am fastidious about tracking these items.

The other consideration in creating a culture of accountability is to allow negotiation. Don't let your team creep past the deadline but do let them negotiate the deadline beforehand. Open the space for them to discuss the work in relation to their other priorities and negotiate the deadline if reasonable and possible. Allow them to put their hand up if they are running behind and afraid they might not meet the deadline. The sooner they do this, the better, as you still have options. If you find out about a delay at the last minute, you usually have no options left.

Explain context

Great leaders such as Hannibal, Napoleon and Churchill inspired their troops to dig deep to overcome the enemy and claim victory. But these great acts were driven by a strong command-and-control dynamic. Their soldiers had little choice but to follow orders.

As a famous line from Tennyson's poem 'The Charge of the Light Brigade' goes, 'Theirs not to make reply, theirs not to reason why, theirs but to do and die'. The soldiers in question would not even think to question orders, but blindly charged forward, even when they knew it was likely to their deaths.

In a war setting this form of leadership may be necessary. But in a corporate setting, where lives are rarely on the line, people want to understand the 'why' before they commit to a demanding deadline and the associated heightened stress levels. Nobody wants to waste their time slaving away on an urgent report that they suspect will just end up unread on someone's desk.

Paul Gracey, who is ANZ Director of Printing Systems at HP Printing Systems Australia, feels very strongly about the need for context and fosters a culture of 'why':

> Overall, I think I help people deal with urgency through creating a culture that is 'allowed' to question. Not just to understand any particular task at hand but also the 'why' of what is being requested. This is in contrast to a culture of 'just do it'.
>
> I find that this not only allows the team to understand their work better, but also allows for more self-moderation about what timelines are in play. Creating an environment where anyone in the team is allowed to seek out the 'why' of any task or project can also allow a better way of doing things to come to light that may not have been apparent had the questions about the workload not been asked.
>
> There are of course always those times where the answer may simply be that we just need to get it done, and to a team that has a culture of questioning to understand this can also be a challenge. But having that as the exception rather than the rule means the team are also quick to mobilise if the request is to simply 'get it done'.

So, take the time to tell them why. Encourage them to ask 'Why?' Help them to understand the bigger picture and they will happily get it done when they have to.

Create traction with complex work

One day a question from a participant in our Productive Leadership program got me thinking about a solution to managing more complex work. He had a fairly busy meeting workload, but was pretty organised and managed to stay on top of most of his simple tasks. What was killing him were the more complex pieces of work in his role that he invariably procrastinated and left until the last minute. These tasks were highly valuable but also highly stressful. He also struggled when delegating this more complex work to his team. The following strategy might have helped him and his team.

Every task, simple or complex, has three stages:

1. deadline

2. planning

3. execution.

A simple task, such as sending an email or making a phone call, will usually roll all three of these stages into one.

Complex tasks, such as preparing for a presentation, writing a report or finalising a budget, are a different beast. With complex work, there is a much greater risk that we will procrastinate, leave it until the last minute and run out of time. Whether you are embarking on a piece of complex work yourself or you are delegating this to a team member, you can use the following strategy to make it clearer and easier to manage.[41]

---

[41] It amazes me that often managers don't have the time to delegate work properly in the first place, but find the time to clean up the mess when the work is not done well as a result of poor delegation.

1. The deadline—Make it visible

Even though this feels like the final stage, it is where we should start. Clarify the deadline and make it visible in both of your schedules. For instance, all-day events in your calendar are a great way to show upcoming deadlines. As deadlines are zero-duration milestones rather than activities, we just need to be able to have them in our line of sight, and be aware as we draw closer to them. You could schedule the event into your calendar and invite the appropriate team member, so you both have it clearly showing in your respective calendars. It's a good idea to review your upcoming deadlines as a part of your weekly planning and make sure you're still on track.

2. The planning—Create a thumbnail sketch

Now that the deadline is in place, we need to come right back to now and start planning the task. Suggest that your team schedule no more than 20 minutes to roughly outline the scope of the task—to quickly brainstorm the key components, stages or activities involved. This is what I call a thumbnail sketch.[42] It's a very rough outline and it will help you estimate how much work is involved and clarify how to approach the task. You might do this rough planning together with less experienced team members, as this will give them confidence and facilitate a productive conversation between both of you.

3. The execution—Block out time

Once they have roughly planned the task, your team need to decide when they will protect some time for the actual work. They should now have a better feel for how much time will be

---

[42] Just like an artist might create a thumbnail sketch in the field, but then paint the final picture later in their studio.

needed. This is best blocked out in their calendar, ideally far enough ahead of the deadline to provide some wiggle room if there are delays. Other things will invariably come up, and it always takes longer than we thought. Make sure they plan for this. When they block this time out, they need to protect it and view it as equally important as any meeting in their schedule. The beauty of having created the thumbnail sketch before they do the work is that their mind will begin working on the task in the time between planning and execution.

In this process, the delegator owns the due date, but the delegatee owns the start date. You both own the responsibility to discuss and negotiate everything in between.

Push and pull to inspire action

As I write this, Australia is going through a record hot spell that has led to unprecedented bushfires early in the season. Volunteer firefighters have been battling blazes for months on end, when in most seasons we would only be a few days or weeks into the fire season. These guys are exhausted and forecasts only suggest worse to come. These brave souls are in a state of acute and chronic reactivity, and although this is what they have trained for, it is taking its toll. Not only have lives been lost, but they are just getting more stretched and tired as the days go on.

To keep going in these conditions, they need great leadership that inspires their efforts and motivates them to keep going. But they will also need a reward. This may not come in the form of payment, or even medals from their leaders, although they will likely be awarded many. The true reward will come from the Australian public after it all dies down and hopefully we as a nation will step up to say thank you. Of course, volunteer firefighters don't do this job for the accolades, but they do want to feel that their efforts were worthwhile and that we city slickers appreciate their sacrifices as much as the people in the affected areas.

The same is true of your teams. They want to be inspired by you. They want to be motivated. And they would not mind a reward every now and again. But they will not be inspired if they are constantly working on unnecessarily urgent work that has no impact. They will not feel motivated if they are constantly forced above the line into the reactive zone, with no protection or help from their manager. And they will not keep doing this if there is no recognition of their efforts.

Learn to spot the exceptional efforts your team make when working on urgent deadlines, and reward them.

A word of thanks may be all that is needed. Maybe a small token gift. A team dinner to say well done. Celebrate the wins. In *The Project Book*, Colin D. Ellis suggests that rather than throwing a lavish party at the end of a project, spend money across the life of a project on gifts, morning teas, lunches and outings to celebrate what has been achieved along the way.

Mobilising the troops also takes more than inspiration and thanks. It also requires you to be hard on them when needed, when they need help to get through the really tough parts. Let me put this into context with another story about my thing for climbing big hills. Or more accurately, mountains that do not require equipment to climb them. I am a walker, not a climber, but love to push my extremes, including my fear of heights.[43]

Earlier in the book I related a story about a climb that I did with my son Finn on Lord Howe island. My love of mountain walking started in 2015 when we were travelling around Ireland. Finn loves a challenge and wanted to do a serious hill climb, so I did some research. We were in Kerry at the time, and it turns out that the highest mountain in Ireland, Carrauntoohil, was about 20 kilometres down the road. Some further research turned up a company that ran guided walks to the top, and there were still spaces on the trip scheduled for the next day. This had to be fate!

I booked our places but was regretting it the next morning at 7 am as we approached our meeting point below the mountain. Carrauntoohil is not that big a mountain in world terms — only 1039 metres tall — but from the car park it looked huge. And it was winter, so there was snow from about 700 metres up, and it looked very steep!

Our guide, a local named Piaras (Irish for Pierce), was very experienced and had been climbing the mountain for over 20 years. I told him of my fear of heights, and he said I should be okay, as long as I listened to what he told me and took it one step at a time.

So, off we went. It was going to be a long day, about seven hours of walking, but the sun was shining, and I was excited. We were on a route called Brother O'Shea's Gully, named after the Christian Brother who fell to his death many years before.[44] This involved crisscrossing a slope that was too steep to climb straight up, followed by a scramble to the summit after that.

---

[43] Or rather my fear of falling from them!

[44] This information did not inspire confidence!

The early part of the slope was fine. We were in snow, not deep but slippery. It required us to dig our toes into the snow with every step. The gradient was not too bad, and as it was just a big slope, the height was not too scary. At least at first! As we progressed upwards, the slope started to get a lot steeper, becoming almost vertical at the top. I was the oldest in the group, so was beginning to struggle with my big backpack, and the sudden awareness that if I slipped, I would be rolling several hundred metres to the bottom.

Up to this point Piaras had kept a close eye on me. He was a very gentle man, softly spoken and had this quiet air of authority about him. 'Well done, Dermot', 'Put your foot here like this, Dermot', 'That's the way, well done'. I knew he was in control and trusted him completely.

As we approached the final steep section, I began to lose it. I was exhausted and scared. Everyone in the group had passed me by, as I began to stumble with each step. My son stopped to help me, but Piaras told him to go on. He knew I needed something special to make this last bit. I stopped and fell to my knees to rest for a minute. The slope was so steep at this point that I was almost upright, even though I was resting on my knees!

'GET OFF YOUR KNEES, DERMOT' I suddenly heard. 'YOU WILL NOT GET TO THE TOP ON YOUR KNEES. COME ON, MAN.' This was my soft-spoken guide, Piaras. He was not so soft-spoken now! But his shouting was like a slap in the face for me, and it spurred me into action. I got up on my feet and ran the final few metres to the top. As I collapsed in a heap on the ridge, Piaras came to me and shook my hand. 'Well done, I knew you could do it!' he said. Soft and gentle again.

I saw his leadership on display in those few moments. As we walked he *pulled* me with him with gentle encouragement and confident assurance. But as things got tough for me, and the situation potentially grew dangerous, he knew he needed to mobilise me with a sense of urgency. He quickly switched to a *push* strategy, shouting instructions to cut through my tired and scared thoughts, and get me moving. But as soon as the danger was averted, and our objective achieved, he went back to being encouraging and supportive.

Great leaders read the situation and know what is needed for each person in that moment. They know when to push, and when to pull.

They know how to mobilise people when needed, but also know when this might break them.

Piaras helped me to achieve something great that day. I made the summit of the highest mountain in Ireland. And I made it back down alive! My son told me later that he had experienced the best day of his life. As mentioned earlier, because of this day, Finn and I now have a ritual where we climb a mountain every year. It never gets any less scary for me, but I always do it with Piaras's voice in my ear when things get tough. 'Get off your knees, Dermot.' Such useful words, in so many ways.

Push strategies should be used with care. Push hard when necessary but keep an eye on the impact of this. Use your authority for things such as hard deadlines purposefully but sparingly. Pull strategies create such a nice balance to the push, and should be used more liberally. Providing context, understanding where your team are at and leading with compassion all go a long way when mobilising people. Oh, and leading from the front by getting stuck in yourself sometimes can also send a great message.

Deal with urgency fatigue

When we drive our teams forward with a sense of urgency, we need to be very sensitive to when it gets to be too much.[45] Working above the line in the reactive zone is good for short periods of time, but when the reactivity starts to become chronic, urgency fatigue can set in.

When this happens, we need to know when and how to bring people back down into the active zone. Divers have gauges to tell them how much air they have left in the tank and when they need to head back to the surface. We need something similar.

The first key to spotting urgency fatigue is awareness.

Know when you are pushing people hard and be on the lookout for signs that it's time to come back down for a while.

Here are some signs that things are getting too much and people have been in the reactive zone for too long:

- everything is urgent and the language used in meetings becomes urgent

- work and information need to be chased up constantly

- people who are normally proactive in their approach become reactive

- balls get dropped and mistakes get made too often

---

[45] Some organisations actively push their people as hard as possible. One term I have heard used to describe this is 'squeezing the asset'. Not very compassionate!

- the team are working longer hours to catch up on their 'real' work

- you lose good people unexpectedly and for reasons that don't seem to stack up

- the volume of email increases at night and on the weekend

- teams are too busy to collaborate on important projects.

Look for the telltale signs in meetings, in conversations and at team offsites.

Your ability to spot the signs of urgency fatigue and intervene can make the difference between retaining a long-term productive team member and someone having a breakdown or resigning due to the constant pressure.

Once you spot signs of urgency fatigue, you need to deal with it. You need to understand what is happening. Is the reactivity being experienced valid? Are you at a point of the project where everything is on track and momentum has been achieved? If so, maybe the pressure can be taken off a bit without any negative impact on the project.

Are there other competing priorities that are causing stress than can be managed differently to relieve pressure? Are there other resources that can be called in to help? Does the person or team involved just need a short break to relieve the pressure and catch their breath before ramping up again?

These strategies might sound familiar. If you flick back to chapter 5, where we cover negotiating urgency, you will see that the dials that we use there to negotiate urgency are the same tools you can use here to relieve the pressure. Your job as manager is to spot urgency fatigue when it happens, and then tweak the right dials to moderate the urgency and relieve the unproductive pressure.

URGENCY PLAYBOOK
PRINCIPLE 9

COMMIT FULLY WHEN
IT IS TRULY URGENT

When a truly urgent issue or opportunity comes along, commit fully in your response by adjusting your existing priorities and refocusing your attention on the new priority.

So much of what we are talking about here is about minimising the impact of unnecessary urgency. But what about the truly urgent things that do require instant attention? In this scenario, we need to commit fully to the response and make it our number one priority.

This requires a mix of decisiveness and flexibility:

- decisiveness to make a firm and quick decision about the best next step

- flexibility to create the space for the urgent work.

Having a system in place that clearly shows your commitments and priorities can help with this. When things change you need to be able to reprioritise and reschedule work to make space. And when things calm down again you need to be able to get back on track and pick up where you left off. A good planning system will help with this.

When we work reactively and operate in firefighting mode most of the time, it is hard to fully commit to the truly urgent. We commit in a shallow way, and can often do more damage and create more rework than necessary.

CHAPTER 10
Defuse

And finally we are in the *defuse* quadrant of the urgency matrix (see figure 10.1, overleaf).

Sometimes, despite all of our good intentions, we get caught up in what I call an 'urgency loop'. This is a state of frenzied activity where everything seems more pressing and critical than it actually is. We end up reacting to stuff unnecessarily, boxing shadows in our own minds. This reactivity in turn leads us to drop the ball on other priorities that themselves become urgent, and so it all spirals downwards. This can happen to an individual or it can happen to a team. It can become the culture of a whole organisation.

You need to be able to defuse these urgency loops when you see them happening. As a team leader, you are the one who needs to drive how urgency is managed by the team. And if you are dealing with a bunch of headless chickens running around the office, you need to calm it down and reinstate order.

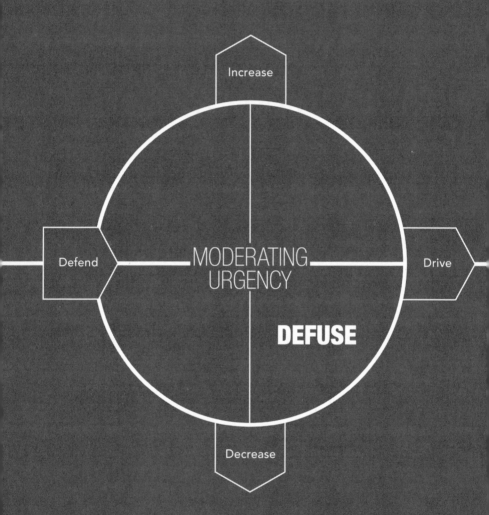

Figure 10.1: the urgency matrix: defuse

Set the right example

Paramedics are taught to always walk into the scene of an emergency. Never run, never rush. No matter how many are injured, or how horrific the scene, they will always walk purposefully onto the scene. This behaviour ensures that a couple of things happen.

Firstly, it allows them time to assess the situation and the environment. They need time to work out what is going on, and also assess any dangers to themselves or the people involved. If they are not fully present to the whole scene, they might miss the fact that it is a hostage situation, or that there is a tree at risk of falling on the victims. Walking in slowly gives them time to look around and absorb the scene holistically.

The second benefit of this approach is that it communicates leadership in what is probably a very charged situation. They need to be the embodiment of calm and authority. Everyone else will panic if it looks like the paramedics are panicked.

As managers, we need to ensure that we carry ourselves in the same purposeful but calm way. We need to create and lead a culture that has a bias towards proactivity. So there are times when we need to defuse the unproductive urgency that we see happening in our own teams.

In a presentation on team productivity I asked the group to recall a leader they had worked with, and to identify a quality that stood out and made them a great leader. One participant recalled an old boss and said, 'No matter how busy he was, he always had time for you'.

What an excellent quality. This is such a great example of what leadership should be. As a leader, you and your behaviours are visible to everyone. Think about how many people that leader inspired over the years, because he always seemed to have time. That ability to 'seem to always have time' would not have come easily. It would have taken work. But it was work worth doing, as it had such a leveraging effect on his team, some of whom went on to become leaders in their own right. And hopefully they went on to display the same quality in their own leadership journey.

Are you a part of the problem? Do you create unnecessary urgency for your team?

The first consideration when defusing urgency must be that you lead by example and set the right tone for your team. You cannot expect them to work proactively if you are the one creating the reactivity in the first place. They need to see you as having a bias for proactivity, and they need to trust that you are not always the person to throw last-minute hand grenades into their plan for the day or week.

This requires you to be organised. It requires you to plan and anticipate. It requires you to adopt all of the principles discussed in part II (on minimising personal reactivity). An inconvenient truth, eh? Yes, you may be a part of the problem, when you should be a part of the solution.

The first principle in the Urgency Playbook is 'don't cry wolf'. This is especially important when you are the manager. You will lose respect and trust quickly if you constantly push for urgency when it's not needed. If people break their backs to deliver something in a short time and then it just sits in your inbox, you are sure to build a sense of resentment within the team.

Calm it down

The phrase 'it all went pear shaped' was much used in Ireland when I was young. There are a few different perspectives on its origin, but the most common one was from the British air force in the post World War II period. When trainee pilots were asked to perform a loop the loop, it was deemed to have gone 'pear shaped' if they could not create the perfect circle. The circle was likely to be bigger at bottom than the top, like the shape of a pear.

One day I was running training for a client in the city. Pretty straightforward. I set my alarm for 6 am and gave myself plenty of time to get into the city for a 9 am start. Unfortunately, traffic was heavy, but having given myself plenty of time, I arrived early enough to not be concerned. The building was just across the road from the car park, so there was even time to grab a quick takeaway coffee on the way. Or so I thought!

As I got out of the car at 8.15 am, the calendar on my phone alerted me to the fact that my 8.30 am training was starting in 15 minutes! What? Mistake #1: 90 per cent of my training programs start at 9 am, and I had assumed that this was no different. But the client in this case was running the training as a part of a team offsite, and they wanted an 8.30 am start to allow an early finish so that the team could fly back to their respective states. I had just not picked this up, which was a big lesson. I and my assistant should have highlighted the exception, to make sure that I did not make stupid assumptions about my schedule.

I was flustered, but I thought I would still make it on time. I would have to forgo my coffee, but I would survive. So, I headed to reception on level 14 and asked them to alert my contact that I had arrived. A few minutes later I got a call on my mobile. It was Melinda, the team director, asking if I was in the city office or the North Sydney office.

OMG! I was in the wrong office! How could this happen? Mistake #2.

Honestly, this sort of pear-shaped fiasco has only happened to me twice in 20 years. My team and I manage hundreds of training events every year and we are normally spot on. But this time, something had gone wrong. Who was to blame was not of importance at the moment; it was all about fixing the problem as quickly and effectively as possible.

So, Melinda, who was so calm and reassuring, suggested I hop on a train to North Sydney, which would be quicker than driving. I agreed and off I went. But here is the key. I did not panic. I did not rush. In fact, I stopped this time and quickly grabbed that takeaway coffee. I walked briskly but calmly to the station and hopped on the next train. I forced myself not to rush and not get stressed.

You see, what Melinda needed most from me was to get there as quickly as possible, but not in a state of stress and panic. She needed me calm and focused for the training ahead, and I think was happy if it took five minutes longer for me to arrive in a state that would ensure I could immediately engage the group and deliver on my brief.

Although a part of me wanted to run and rush to mitigate the problem I had caused, this would not have served the situation. Responding to the situation rather than reacting to it allowed me to arrive in a reasonable state, have a laugh with the team about how ironic it was that a time management expert was late to his own training, and then get stuck in to delivering a session that would boost their productivity.

Reactivity is a response to urgency. But it is one of many responses that we can choose. Stress and worry can often cloud our decision-making. As the Dalai Lama once said: 'If something is stressing you and you can do something about it, then do it and don't worry. If you cannot do anything about it, then don't worry also.'

When your team are in a state of panic, you may need to calm them or the situation down. It has been said that the best way to refocus a person in a state of panic is to slap them in the face. This panic-slap creates a circuit breaker in their thought patterns and brings their thinking back into focus. Please *do not* slap your team.[46] But I reckon that you do need a figurative slap in the face for these situations.

Have a chat to your team about the idea of the panic-slap. Come up with a phrase or a sign that signifies the panic-slap has been served. This can be a humorous way to cut through and say, 'Hey, this is one of those times we discussed. Let's stop for a moment and reassess.'

Get on the balcony

Once you have identified that the team or a team member is caught up in an urgency loop, you can now refocus their efforts on the real priorities. What is most important in their role is rarely the emails they are reacting to, or even the endless meetings they are attending. That is just the stuff that fills up their inboxes and their schedule. To help them to refocus on what is most important, here's a great strategy.

In the introduction I mention the time I spent working under Professor Ron Heifetz at The Harvard Kennedy School. Ron's

---

[46] I mean that. Not a good thing to do!

work inspired this book and so much of my thinking on urgency.

In his book *Leadership on the Line*, co-written with Marty Linsky, he describes the idea of getting off the dance floor and onto the balcony.

> Few practical ideas are more obvious or more critical than the need to get perspective in the midst of action. Any military officer, for example, knows the importance of maintaining the capacity for reflection, even in the 'fog of war'. Great athletes can at once play the game and observe it as a whole—as Walt Whitman described it, 'being both in and out of the game'. Jesuits called it 'contemplation in action'. Hindus and Buddhists call it 'karma yoga', or mindfulness. We call this skill 'getting off the dancefloor and going to the balcony', an image that captures the mental activity of stepping back in the midst of action and asking 'What's really going on here?'

This is such a powerful idea, but, as they suggest, it's hard to execute when you are in the middle of a hectic day. But with practice, like any mindfulness activity, it can be done in any situation with very little time.

For example, imagine you're in a meeting with some of your team. You notice that one of your team, Lucy, has cut across another team member, Rob, a couple of times, disagreeing with his input. You always make room for robust debate, but these comments seem stronger than normal.

Rather than jumping in and getting involved, take yourself off to the balcony in your mind. What is really happening here? The content of the discussion is not too contentious, and you feel like they can work that out easily enough themselves. But maybe the discussion is being driven by other tensions. In fact, you reflect, Rob and his team have been putting a lot of pressure on Lucy recently because of some looming project deadlines.

Some of the deadlines have slipped due to some poor planning on Rob's part, and Lucy is now bearing the brunt of the fallout.

This reflection leads you to have a couple of one-on-one discussions with each of them offline to resolve the tensions. The project deadlines still need to be met, but some additional resources can be brought in to help Lucy and Rob now knows that his lack of planning is not reasonable.

A senior leader and a wonderful advocate for my training shared a story with me as I researched this book.

> Very recently I was super busy (as per usual) and one of my staff tackled me in the kitchen to ask if I had a spare five minutes to discuss something. I asked if we could push it out to later in the day. Later that afternoon, they stuck their head into my office and asked if now was a good time. I was swamped and asked if it was urgent. The response I got was along the lines of, 'no, not particularly urgent, we can catch up later'. However, it was delivered in a manner that suggested they really wanted to speak with me.
>
> Fortunately, I had enough awareness to pause, bring the individual into my office and have a conversation. It turned out to be a personal health–related matter. The person needed support, encouragement and reassurance from me. It was not 'business' urgent, but personally very important for the individual.
>
> I reflected on this afterward and thought how close I'd come to turning them away, which would have been awful.

It is so easy to miss this dynamic if you are always on the dance floor, in the middle of things. Or worse, if you are always in meetings and not on the dance floor at all.

Try to practise the art of mentally stepping back from time to time to ask 'What is really going on here?'

Don't reward reactivity

Finally, a thought on how your actions might create a more reactive culture. Think about what behaviours you reward or applaud with your team. When one of your team replies instantly to an email from you, does that secretly impress you? Is that another tick in your mind that leads to a promotion for them down the track? When you call a last-minute meeting and one of your team declines because they have another commitment, does that infuriate you? Do you mark them down for that?

There is a risk that you as a manager confuse:

- reactivity with responsiveness
- negotiation with insubordination
- moderation with incompetence.

If you reward reactivity it sets a tone with your team that promotes working reactively. If you only reward proactivity when it does not get in the way of urgent priorities, you also set a tone and create a set of behaviours. And remember, culture is just a set of group behaviours. Reward these.

————

So, there you go. A set of clear strategies to use with your team to moderate this force called urgency:

1. Respond if it is real and reasonable.

2. Absorb if it is not.

3. Mobilise if you need to create traction or momentum.

4. Defuse if you see it taking hold unnecessarily.

Four things you can do. The key is to do something. Because just letting urgency run amok does nothing for the productivity of your team.

URGENCY PLAYBOOK
<u>PRINCIPLE 10</u>

DO WHAT YOU SAY YOU
ARE GOING TO DO

Deliver on your promises and commitments, or at least put your hand up and renegotiate if you cannot deliver as promised. Don't force others to chase you.

All work gets done through a series of next-step actions. And often it's like a tennis match: I hit the ball to you, then you need to return the serve so I can do my next piece and hit it on to someone else, and on it goes.

One of the key causes of urgency is that others commit to completing actions by a certain date, and then they let you down. You end up chasing them for the work (if you remember on time), which raises your stress levels and pushes out your time frames.

What may have started out as a very proactive approach to your work can easily become a reactive game of chasing and prodding to get what you need.

You may not be able to control how others behave, but you can control how you behave. So, make sure you are the one others can depend upon. Do what you say you are going to do but make realistic promises at the same time. I would prefer to work with dependable people who negotiate reasonable time frames with me rather than reactive people who do things immediately for me one day, and then have to be chased another day.

Next steps

Calvin Coolidge once said, 'We cannot do everything at once, but we can do something at once.' A book like this obviously sets out a broad agenda for change, both in your own personal behaviours and in your team culture. It is not the work of one day, nor a quick fix. No matter how committed to reducing unproductive urgency you may be, you will not be able to do everything that is required at once. But you can do *something* at once. This final chapter will help you to work out what that something will be. Where do we start?

Late last year I participated in a powerful mentoring session with two of my long-time mentors, Matt Church and Peter Cook. These blokes have been instrumental in the success of my practice over the past few years, and very instrumental in the fact that I have now written three books.

I kind of feel that my business is in a good place at this stage. My practice is successful and I have achieved reasonably good work–life balance. I am doing work that I am passionate about with clients that I enjoy working with. I have a great team supporting me and fantastic support for what I do at home. So I went into our mentoring session not really knowing what we should focus on, as everything seemed pretty good.

Matt and Peter agreed. My practice was healthy in their eyes. My decision-making seemed sound. My positioning was excellent. But they were interested in me, and what was going on inside. We talked about what my practice might look like over the next ten years, and what going to the next level might look like. And their advice was very simple. Whatever the next level is for me,[47] the journey there starts with a journey into me. Once I work out what the next level is, to get there I will need to grow and evolve. I will need to deeply understand me and what makes me tick. And I will need to grow as a person to be able to step up to that next level.

Don't worry: I'm not suggesting that you need to immediately go on a personal exploration journey to implement the lessons from this book. But I do think sorting out your own backyard is a good place to start.

Start with you

So, the 'something' you could do straight away could be to think about your approach to urgency. Are you reactive by nature? Do you tell yourself stories about your reactivity? Could you learn to work more proactively? What was your personal workstyle score in chapter 2?

Changing your own habits and behaviours takes real commitment and conviction. It is not easy. It can be helpful to be really clear why you are doing it. If this *why* is powerful enough, it will carry you through the hard times. When I climbed Mount Gower on Lord Howe Island I had a powerful

---

[47] And I am still formulating that thought.

why. My son Finn, and the bond that we were creating through this experience, was the *why* I needed as my knuckles were being scraped raw on the cliff, and every fibre in my body screamed to go back to where it felt safe and comfortable.

So, get clear about why making these changes will benefit you. When you are clear about the why, here are a few first steps you could take:

- Review you personal planning systems and ensure they are geared towards proactive planning and activity management.[48]

- Build regular times into your schedule for personal planning.

- Wean yourself off your email and social media addiction.[49]

- Become more mindful and aware of your behaviours and reactions.

- Talk to your manager and your team and understand how they see your work style.

- Schedule a reminder to review your progress in three months and every three months after that. This will be an ongoing path to mastery.

- Don't be too hard on yourself when you fall off the wagon.

- Reward yourself when you see a change.

---

[48] Stop piling your work up in your inbox and your to-do list and start scheduling your actions in a dated task list or calendar.

[49] I wish I had invented a patch for this—I would make a million!

Then your team

Next look up and think about the team around you. How did your work environment score in the questionnaire in chapter 2? How do they work and what control or influence do you have in shifting the team culture? If you are a manager, you definitely have some control in this regard and are in the perfect position to help moderate the urgency your team faces. You can be instrumental in creating a new team 'micro-culture' that resets the way things are done around here, at least by *your* team. But even if you are not the team manager, you should be in a position to influence how those around you work. You may not have formal authority that comes from positional power, but you do have informal authority that is built through experience, good influencing skills and the respect that comes from demonstrating good personal behaviours around urgency.

To start on the journey to creating a more proactive team culture, try the following:

- Raise this as a topic at your next team meeting or offsite.

- Tell your team how you are going to work moving forward and raise their awareness around the importance of moderating urgency.

- Share the Urgency Playbook with the team and agree to put the principles in place for a three-month trial period.

- Look out for opportunities to protect your team from unproductive urgency.

- Openly discuss the times when you need to drive urgency and why it is necessary.

- Get up on the balcony from time to time and try to spot when the team is working in the reactive zone too much.

- Agree to change the language in the team from reactive to proactive.[50]

And finally ... your organisation

If you are a people leader in your organisation, this is a conversation you should be having with your leadership team. The benefits of creating a more proactive culture across the organisation are many. But this requires real cultural change, across many people and over a long period of time. This takes leadership.[51]

Creating this sort of cultural change across your organisation takes people, resources and probably some budget. But mostly it takes a sense of priority from the leadership team. I know that when I put my gaze on an issue or opportunity, great things happen. The challenge is that many things are vying for my gaze, and my time and energy are limited resources. So are yours. So there will be an opportunity cost to committing to this shift. What are you willing to sacrifice to put your gaze on this project? Understanding this can help you to commit fully to this, and to drive it home to its full conclusion.

I saw this happen with Paul Gracey at HP, whom I mention in chapter 9. He put his gaze very firmly on the issue of email noise within his team, and over a 12-month period worked to shift their culture around email. After just 12 months, he felt that the way his team used email had changed substantially.

---

[50] Terms such as ASAP and urgent are not helpful in most situations.

[51] But if you have bothered to read this paragraph, you are probably a leader, so all good.

If you want to create a cultural change around urgency in your organisation, try taking the following steps:

- Put this topic on the agenda for your next leadership team offsite.[52]

- Mobilise a handpicked team of internal champions with a sense of urgency around this project.

- Look at your key clients, suppliers and stakeholders and work out if they are a part of the problem or a part of the solution.

- Talk about your urgency culture at your next conference or large team gathering.

- Demonstrate exemplary personal behaviours around urgency at all times.

- Commit to rewarding the right behaviours in your team.

Then the world!

No, only joking. I reckon you've done enough! We will never eradicate urgency, nor would we want to. But hopefully we can tame it a bit, and reduce the unproductive urgency in our workplaces.

My wish for you is that you are energised and galvanised to take action. That you have a clear first step, and some sense that you could make a difference for yourself and those around you.

Good luck on your journey. As they say in Ireland, may the road rise up to meet you, and the wind be always at your back.[53]

---

[52] After giving everyone on the leadership team a copy of this book, of course.

[53] And if you see an Irish farmer out standing in his field, say hi from me!

Index